Life

Changing

Poems

Book Eight

**BY
JIM PEMBERTON**

JIM PEMBERTON

First Edition

Cover and Interior Design by Cindy Bauer

ISBN: 9781691865543
Imprint: Independently published

Printed in the United States of America

To my wonderful wife, Denise.

I'd also like to thank Phil and Judy Walser, Dan and Betty Fitzsimmons, Ward Caretti and Pastor Ricky Lowe for their prayers and support over the years.

LIFE CHANGING POEMS - BOOK EIGHT

I Love Jesus first Of All!

I really love Jesus the first of all!
He answered when I gave him a call!

I called out to him in prayer some time ago.
He came and redeemed my sinful soul.

I'm so glad for the opportunity freely given!
I've been set free and totally forgiven!

Won't you give Jesus a call from your heart?
On your knees in prayer is a good place to start!

Jesus Lifted Me Up!

Jesus totally blessed and lifted me up!
Now, each day, his love fills me up!

It wasn't I, but him that found me.
Now, each day, his love surrounds me.

His hope blesses and gives me strength.
His grace is an immeasurable length!

I'm honored and glad to know him.
I want all to know how much I love him!

Thank You Jesus For all You done!

Thank you Jesus for all you done!
You've overcome! The victory's won!

Satan's a foe that's been defeated.
With you as my Lord, I'm now completed.

You've done so much for me, I can't express.
You've brought to my life peace and rest.

I honor and bring worship to your name.
I'm glad you're here and that you came!

Jesus Changed My Old Life!

Jesus changed me and the sins of the past.
He brought a joy and peace that lasts!

He brought to me life and joy eternal.
I know now my name's in heaven's journal!

Thanks to him, I have life everlasting.
His life for mine is what he was asking.

I'm so glad for the choice that I made.
There's nothing for Jesus that I would trade!

Delight In Jesus!

There's many things that get us excited.
It's common to get happy and delighted.

There's many things that "turn someone on."
Often, people don't know, "right from wrong."

There's a satisfaction that on Jesus brings.
No matter how hard we try "other things."

There's a satisfaction Jesus that can be found.
No matter if you're on "the wrong side of town."

Only he brings opportunity and love divine.
He is faithful, and has stood the test of time.

Won't you come and accept his delight today?
Above all else, he remains the ONLY way!

Let's come together and worship his lovely name!
Once he touches us, we'll never be the same!

Taking delight in Jesus is the best place to be.
He brings everlasting life for all eternity!

I Love Jesus first Of All!

I really love Jesus the first of all!
He answered when I gave him a call!

I called out to him in prayer some time ago.
He came and redeemed my sinful soul.

I'm so glad for the opportunity freely given!
I've been set free and totally forgiven!

Won't you give Jesus a call from your heart?
On your knees in prayer is a good place to start!

Getting Closer To God

One thing we need to know most assuredly.
As a Christian, we need Godly maturity.

We need to have a Holy Spirit's discernment.
Let's be filled with God's love not discouragement...

Time for prayer and Bible reading must be spent.
As your commitment to Christ must be 100 percent.

We can "pretend" to be God's child, and act "cool."
But it's God that we can never fool.

Take a stand for Jesus "in a world gone wrong."
For though we are weak. Christ remains strong.

We don't know what tomorrow will bring.
That's why living for Jesus is the most important thing.

Let's make a decision for him all of the way.
He'll never disappoint us now... Or any day!

Am I Spending My Time For God?

The longer I live... I think of how short life is.
The older I get, the more I know God lives.

The most important truth that I know...
Is a savior who's brought health and salvation to my soul.

I think about what's important to me...
The questions remains; "where will I spend eternity?"

Many I knew have since passed away...
So I want to live for God until my final day.

I often think and begin to see....
I need more of Jesus, and less of me!

The longer I live, it's evident and revealing...
The return of our Lord and his glorious appearing!

The longer I live, is God's way of giving me another chance...
To allow him to be Lord... Over every circumstance!

The longer I live, is another day to enjoy being forgiven...
Jesus is with me each day that I'm livin'!

The Joy Of Jesus

The Joy of Jesus is a blessing to behold.
It's unspeakable and the half isn't told.

It's a joy most enduring and wonderful.
It brings abundant life so fruitful.

Won't you experience this joy yourself?
I've been blessed to know this myself.

The joy of Jesus is a treasure worth knowing.
Jesus gives it in abundance life overflowing!

His joy is precious and worth the cost!
It comes from victory over

The Treasure Of Jesus

The treasure of Jesus is worth the cost.
He traded his life for ours on the cross!

We're more precious to him than gold.
More valuable than what can be told.

The treasure of knowing him is sweet delight.
He's here to help us each day and night!

Won't you accept this eternal treasure today?
Where there's a willing heart, he makes a way!

He brings more to your life than you'll ever know!
In him, can you be made complete and whole!

The treasure he gives, all the money cannot buy!
It'll be an eternal treasure long after you die!

To live is Christ. To die is a valuable gain.
We can find all that we need in Jesus' name!

The Lord's Mercy Shines Bright!

The Lord is good and his mercy shines bright!
He has come and brought me pure delight!

He's wonderful and his wonders to perform.
He keeps me safe from life's fiercest storms!

He's marvelous and is majesty reigns supreme!
He is God over all and can do anything!

Let's receive his mercy why we have the time.
Let's allow is grace to purify our minds!

Let's allow his love to keep our hearts strong.
It's in God's tender hands where we all belong!

I bless and thank the Lord for all that he's done1
All praise to God the father, spirit and son!

Jesus, I'm Grateful For You!

Jesus, I'm blessed and grateful for you!
I don't know what I'd do without you!

You came and gave me hope and meaning,
You salvation and love, I began receiving!

You brought me peace when it wasn't around.
Your spirit put my life on higher ground!

You gave me a joy that's full and unspeakable!
Whatever my sin, it's never "unreachable."

Thank you Jesus for everything you've given!
Now I can live, with the joy of being forgiven!

Jesus Can Make Things Right!

There's so much wrong in the world today!
Only Jesus can make the darkness go away!

Only he can bring peace to a stormy sea.
Only He provides hope for all eternity!

Jesus can make everything work for the best!
It's only in him that we find comfort and rest!

I invite you to come now and really trust him!
Where would we be if we didn't have him?

Jesus fulfills All Our Dreams!

Jesus fulfills all of our desires and dreams!
We can put our faith in him for everything!

He is the only one who's forever loyal and true!
All he does is because of his love for me and you!

Knowing him brings peace and satisfaction.
Inviting him as your lord is true love in action!

Won't you accept and trust him to help you?
He's here now and wants a relationship with you!

Let's Focus On The Purity of Jesus!

While this world flaunts perverted sexuality…
We need to focus on God's true identity!

We need to seek the purity God tells us about!
We need to read and study his word throughout!

Let's focus on that which is lovely and pure.
Only Jesus can give a life that's eternally secure.

The purity and sweetness of Jesus is like no other!
It's the same kind of love that touches one another!

If you're having thoughts of an ungodly kind…
Please come to Jesus, while you have the time!

Allow his words of life come and touch you!
He'll do so much because he loves and wants you!

Jesus is the same yesterday and never will change!
Behold our wonderful Lord and his mighty name!

If You Don't Forgive

How can you make heaven, if you don't forgive?
What kind of example, for Christ, will you give?

"Not having anything to do with him," is the name.
You have no one else, but you, to put the blame.

You're sins aren't forgive, if you can't do this task.
Is it too much to do what Jesus simply asks?

He gave his life for the atonement of our sins.
This is where true freedom in him truly begins!

Time is short! We need to make the best of it!
Jesus has heard your excuses, and he's tired of it!

Lay your grudges and hard feelings at the altar.
Don't let your heart to get like the "Rock of Gibraltar."

Scripture reminds us clearly to LOVE ONE ANOTHER!
Let's walk in love and forgive our sister and brother!

I Love Jesus, Yes I do!

I love Jesus, yes I surely do!
I love him, what about YOU?

I appreciate him and all he does.
I give him my heart, life and love!

I'm thankful for grace divine!
He cleansed and renewed my mind!

He can change you, if you let him.
Please come and don't forget him!

He's faithful and remains the same!
All that we need, is in his name!

I'm complete In Jesus!

With Jesus on board, I'm complete!
He fills my life, from my head to feet!

He came and his love daily surrounds me!
It wasn't I, but his Spirit that found me!

He brought a wholeness I never had.
Now I'm redeemed, joyful and glad!

I bless his name and hold him so dear!
He calms all my worries and fears!

The strength he gives is like no other!
He sticks my closer than a brother!

Anything I ever need, I have in HIM!
I thank him so much again and again!

Jesus Gives Me Living Water and My Daily Bread

Because of Jesus, I've been daily fed.
I receive the living water and daily bread.

He gives what I need and so much more.
It's his sweet presence I treasure and adore.

His spirit gives the strength that I need.
His word is what I think about and read.

His water quenches and nourishes my soul.
His bread satisfies and makes me whole!

I'm so thankful of what he gives me.
Each day now, his joy is what fills me!

Glory to God! Jesus brings glory divine!
I'm enjoying his love one day at a time!

Jesus, Anyone Could Fall In Love with You!

Jesus, anyone could fall in love with you
It happened to me. I know it's true.

You're someone that I treasure and adore.
It's always YOU that I need more and more!

It's in you, Jesus, that I take sweet delight.
You're here to help me through a dark night.

Your presence is like a sweet ocean breeze.
I come before you and bow on my knees.

I confess my sins and give you praise!
I want to be with you all of my days.

I want my past to be put behind me.
It was the love of Jesus that has found me!

Enjoying YOU Jesus is the best I can do!
Where would I be, if not for YOU?

Enjoy The Lord's Goodness!

Come and enjoy the Lord's goodness today!
Come and listen to what God has to say?

Taste of his goodness that flows within.
Taste of his sweet love again and again!

Trust in him for his promises so true.
Trust him for all the things he wants to do!

Enjoy the life giving power of Jesus' name!
Enjoy how your life can be CHANGED!

Witness the power of his life changing blood!
Witness the glory of his awesome eternal love!

Today can be the day for Jesus to touch you!
Today can be the time for God to transform you!

Will God Forgive Me?

I have problems and sin! There are many.
Is there any hope for me? Is there ANY?
I've brought to my family a lot of shame.
I'm often embarrassed when others call my name.
Past failures and mistakes. They abound!
And have a tendency to "pull me down."

I've often felt "unlovable" with a discouraged mind.
It seems like my life, "is racing against time."
I heard that Jesus loves me and can make me whole.
How could someone like this love me? I'll never know.
How could a God who's so merciful and lovable...
Find anything inside of me... That's "valuable?"

I've read in God's word, that Jesus traded my life with his!
An abundant and eternal life... Jesus freely gives! I ask you,
Jesus, to come into my life and wash it clean.
I invite you to be my Lord. Over everything!
I know that I've often stumbled and sinned!
I need your presence and peace within!

Only YOU can restore my life through your gift of salvation.
I give you my heart... And an open invitation!
Thank you Lord! For the work that you're going to do.
I want you to know how much I love and need YOU!

God Beautifully Created Us!

God beautifully created us with our "unique features."
Because of sin, we've become "fallen creatures."

God deigned us to have fellowship with him!
But that was broken, on account of SIN!

God formed us out of the dust of the ground…
His wonderful creation was made all around!

God had a purpose and a plan in mind.
He wanted to be a part of mankind.

This was broken because of Adam and Eve's fall.
But through Christ, he made a way for all!

Through Christ we have access to God's throne.
He died for us so we can make heaven our home!

His gift of mercy is for all to receive!
Won't you accept him and believe?

Look To Jesus!

Have you been frustrated with
"church and religion?"
By the "superficial" hope
and man-focused attention?

Have you been "cast out"
by a fellow church member?
The faults you have...
They do remember.

Some in church who pray
and worship on Sunday.
Are often a different person
come Monday.

Some who claim to be
"righteous and holy."
Are simply full of
"hot air and baloney."

Look to Jesus!
Look beyond the "church crowd."
Read his holy word...
And shout it out loud!

A relationship with Jesus
is the most important thing.
Into your life...
His righteousness he will bring.

The "religious distractions"
will simply go.
Once Christ has control
over your thoughts and soul.

He's the answer!
His word 100% true.
You're precious to him...
How much he loves YOU!

Do You Feel Helpless?
Jesus Is Here!

Do you feel like you're
"worn out" and defeated?
Like nothing in your life
has really been completed?

Do you feel like your life
is going "downhill" fast?
Do you wonder how much longer
you're "going to last?"

Do you feel like you've hit too
many bumps in the road?"
The weight upon your shoulders
feels like a "heavy load?"

Do you feel like you
just can't take it anymore?
You may wonder if anything in
life is worth living for...

There's good news
that I have to bring!
I can tell you of someone
who can take care of everything!

His name is Jesus,
and he can change your life today!
He is God, and can take
all your problems away!

Why not allow him to change
your life throughout?
This is what HIS love
is really all about!

You can experience
the power of God within?
You can to be forgiven
and born again!

If this is what you want
and what your heart wants to gain.
Simply reach out to Jesus
and call on his name…

God Gives Peace
For Our Struggles Within

I was talking with someone
who had many struggles within.
He said he "couldn't help
giving in to sin."

He talked about the many kind of things
he's been going through.
He was very discouraged.
And didn't know what to do.

Phillipians 4:8 was the verse
that came to my mind.
That which is lovely and good…
He should find!

He acknowledged the truth
of what God's word said.
He said he "was going to clean house."
Before he went to bed.

It was just a few weeks later
that I met him at church.
He had a desire for more of God.
And a new "search."

As he searched God's word,
he found the help he needed.
"God please help and forgive me,"
were the words he pleaded.

He reached "rock bottom."
With no way out.
And discovered what living for Christ
is all about!

He began to have victory
in areas of life he never had.
God had given him his hope and love.
He is so glad!

As he came closer to Jesus,
his life has a new meaning.
Into the arms of his savior,
he is leaning!

He knows what
the power of Christ can do!
And found hope in the words of Christ,
"I LOVE YOU!"

Won't you accept the gift from God,
this person received?
Find out what it's like
to trust God and believe!

What In Life, Are You Looking For?

What is it in life,
you're looking for?
You have a purpose in life
And much more!

Life's goals and ambitions
are many!
But deep down inside, you
may be feeling "empty."

If it's pleasure and success
you wish to obtain...
You'll find what you need
in Jesus' name!

Everything you'll need,
you can find in him!
Through his blood,
a new life begins!

Won't you accept his grace
and mercy divine?
He's very patient,
forgiving and kind!

He provides for your needs!
So don't forget...
His love has never let go
of YOU yet!

In Bondage

I know that it's easy to get discouraged and upset.
Being in bondage... But you can't escape "just yet."

You've tried "everything." And don't know what else to do.
Often wondering if there's "anyone" who can "help you through."

The things you've done. You asked God to forgive.
Yet struggle with this Each day you live.

You go to church and put on a big "smile."
And wonder if living is really "worth the while."

You have run for prayer time and time again.
And yet constantly struggle with this habitual sin.

So many times when you've tried to call on Jesus' name.
Yet find yourself in another sea of "guilt and shame."

Jesus is here now and really wants you to know.
Everything in your life. You must completely let go.

Start today by not thinking of things done in the past.
Come to Jesus now! He'll give you true joy that will LAST!

There is another thing you must do. You really should!
Begin to think on things which are wholesome and good!

Allow God to bring to your life the needed victory now!
He'll make you a brand new person! And HOW!

I Know Of An Old Fashioned Family!

There's a family I know,
that may seem old fashioned.
But they serve others
from a heart of compassion!

They don't have much in the scope
of entertainment.
But they had each other,
and much contentment.

They have a love for God
that comes from within!
They're thankful to the Lord
for being their friend!

They don't get too involved
with what the world brings.
They have each other's love.
They have everything!

This family has been
an inspiration to others too!
By their giving hearts,
in much of what they do!

This family has a commitment
to serve God above.
And have asked Jesus
to fill them with his love!

This may seem old fashioned,
not to have a lot of things…
But they know their Lord
and the love that he brings!

I'm thankful to know them
and their Godly inspiration…
I extend to them a heart
of thanks and appreciation!

Please dear Lord,
bless and keep them in your arms!
Be with them Jesus,
and protect them from harm!

May the blessings of God
keep flowing through them!
May the peace and joy of God
continue to be with them!

America Needs To Return To God!

There's something that I find kind of "odd."
This country's drifted far from God.

Many talk about a God and state separation.
Courts try to remove him from this nation.

It seems like it takes a tragedy for about him.
Yet, there's remains those who still doubt him.

This life we all have is special and God given!
Through Christ, can we have our sins forgiven.

Before this day is over, we can have this assurance…
Having our sins cleansed is the best life insurance!

Let's all return to God, before it's too late!
One day soon, we'll have an eternal fate!

It's time to wake up the evil around us!
Remember it was God's love that found us!

Coming before God in repentance is the best!
Only through Jesus, we can be blessed!

Only Jesus can give true hope and security!
Only he can give eternal love in eternity!

Through Christ, can we overcome the evil tide.
Only in Christ, can we be on the winning side!

Many In Church Have Compromised God's Holy word!

There's scripture that many in church say doesn't apply.
They'd rather turn God's truth into a corruptible lie.

It appears that many in church want what "soothes them."
They live a compromised life that truly fools them!

They want to make as many "friends" as they can.
Righteous and holy living, they don't understand.

Many in church no longer want to seek God's way.
They'd rather listen to what others have to say!

Preachers with "itching ears," is what they seek…
Meanwhile, they're spiritually blind and weak!

It's time to stand up for God and his way of living!
Think about God's holy truth and what he's giving!

He's given his words of life, to daily guide us!
He's given his Holy Spirit to be here beside us!

Believing and living 100% by God's word is the key!
If you want God's abundant life and victory!

We Need God's Righteousness and Holiness Now!

A person was raised in church as a young man.
He was involved with worship and a gospel band.

Then one day, he seemed to have a "new" conversion."
He bragged about his "new" life of ungodly perversion.

This kind of thing is happening all over the place.
It seems like anything falls under "love and grace."

What happened to the churches in this nation today?
Have we forgotten what God's word has to say?

What do many of us come to a church service for?
What happens the moment we enter the door?

Are we here to seek man's approval in what we believe?
What kind of filth and lies have people in church received?

God's purpose in his word, is to help us overcome!
He's given us victory through the sacrifice of his son!

Jesus is coming back for a bride without spot or blemish!
Without his holiness in our life, we'll one day perish!

Let's come before our Lord in repentance and sorrow!
Let's do it today! Jesus could come tomorrow!

What Is Friendship?

Have you thought about what friendship is?
Is it someone who loves and forgives?
I'm sure many people have a different meaning!
There's many directions to be leaning.

Friendship comes in different forms and kinds.
It develops a kinship among hearts and minds!
I'm sure that many want to be a friend to another.
But there is one, who sticks closer than a brother!

This one is the very best friend, that I can speak of!
He brings the best friendship, that I can think of!
He brings to friendship a new purpose and desire…
To bring eternal love! And lift you up higher!

He is the very definition of what a friend should be!
He'll be your best friend now! And for eternity!
His name is Jesus! I encourage you to invite him in!
Won't you allow him to be your savior and friend?

His faithfulness and commitment are 100% true!
He'll always be there for me, and for YOU!
Friendship with Jesus, is fellowship divine!
He'll never let you down! Not a single time!
Friendship with Jesus… Without a doubt!
He is what being a true friend is all about!

Jesus Is Always Your Best Friend!

Have you thought about what friendship is?
Is it someone who loves and forgives?
Many people have a different meaning!
There's many directions to be leaning.

Friendship comes in different forms and kinds.
It develops a kinship among hearts and minds!
Many want to be a friend to another.
But there's one, who sticks closer than a brother!

He's the very best friend, that one can speak of!
He brings the best friendship, that one can think of!
He brings to friendship a new purpose and desire...
To bring eternal love and lift you up higher!

He's the very definition of what a friend should be!
He'll be your best friend now and for eternity!
His name is Jesus! I encourage you to invite him in!
Won't you allow him to be your savior and friend?

His faithfulness and commitment are 100% true!
He'll always be there for me, and for YOU!
Friendship with Jesus, is fellowship divine!
He'll never let you down! Not a single time!

Friendship with Jesus... Without a doubt!
He's what being a true friend is all about!

What Happened to Our Churches???

Someone talked about being in church as a young man.
He was involved with worship and a "Christian" band.

But then he talked about having a "conversion."
He shared about his "new" proud life of perversion.

Isn't this any wonder that it's happening more and more?
What in the world are the churches really here for?

Preaching on anything on holiness seems to be of the past.
People are looking for "fake" love that will never last!

Where's the conviction in the services you're attending?
Are you a real child of God? Or someone who's pretending?

Going to a church must be more than a "Sunday thing."
You need to follow Jesus and give him everything!

This man made religion we have is downright disgusting!
It's not a building, but in Christ alone we must be trusting!

Jesus is coming back for a bride without wrinkle or blemish!
If you're not ready for his coming, you will one day perish!

Let's come and repent of our sin in humble confession!
Let's make Jesus our number one prize and possession!

Let's seek his holiness and his life changing power!
Let's do it today! He could come this very hour!

Have You Talked To Jesus Today?

What would you sacrifice, if it meant an answered prayer?
What would you tell Jesus, in your moment of despair?

If you talked to Jesus now, what words would you use?
Talking with him... What have you to lose?

Would you be willing to give all you have to HIM today?
Will he be the one you trust when you take time to pray?

HE's here now! He's patient, loving and willing to listen.
Without him, there's so much in life that you're missin'!

Won't you take the time to give him your whole heart?
Spending time alone with him is a great place to start!

Don't let the many distractions in life try to fool you!
He died on the cross, because he loves you!

This can be the time for your prayer to be given!
By Jesus' blood, you can be blessed and forgiven!

Allow the presence of Jesus to come and make you whole!
Through his grace, he'll strengthen your weary soul!

Getting alone with Jesus in prayer is the best place to be!
He'll help you to overcome and give you the victory!

Jesus, There's Nothing As Precious As You!

Jesus… There's nothing as precious as you!
There's no one who's so faithful and true!
There's nothing as beautiful as your love for me!
I love you and want to be with you for all eternity!

There's nothing that compares with your beauty untold.
None of this world's riches,   it's silver or gold!
Your glory reigns above and is supreme!
You're the Lord over the earth and everything!

I need your touch, that I may be whole!
I will sing of your praises wherever I go!
May my love for you be focused into a new direction.
I celebrate the power of your glorious resurrection!

My soul longs for you, as in a dry and thirsty land.
Behold all of the wonderful works, from your hands!
May you be lifted up in everything I do!
It's my way of showing how I appreciate YOU!

You gave me what I need and much more!
You're the one that I worship and adore!
You've given me a new life that I never had.
You brought comfort and joy. I am so glad!

Thank you my Lord and dearest friend!
To this I say: "Hallelujah" and "Amen!"

Don't Give Up! God Is Here!

Have you been thinking of giving up?
Perhaps you feel like you've had enough?
Have trials in life been getting you down?
Do you feel like there's not a friend around?

I know what it feels like, to be in a difficult situation!
Things in life can change, with no explanation!
I know of a God who listens and hears you!
Won't you trust him? He's always with you!

Won't you give him a chance to help you recover?
There's an abundant life in him, that you can discover!
He's what you really need at this time!
He's always loving, patient and very kind!

Won't you come and bring your needs to him?
Confess your every need, and come before him!
His love can pick you up and bring hope today!
He cares and loves you more, than words can say!

I'm Glad I Trusted Jesus!

Jesus has done so much for me!
He removed my sins! I Am Free!

He's done more than I could ask.
He helps me when I face a difficult task.

He's done more than I could ever do.
He's changed my life and made me brand new!

He's done these things and much more!
He's done more than I could ask for!

He's doing a complete work in my life.
He removed all pain, sorrow and strife!

He's doing many beautiful things!
He gives happiness only he can bring!

He's here and waiting for us all!
Won't you take time to give him a call?

As It Was In Noah's Day!

A very evil and wicked generation this is becoming!
God's word warns us that his judgment is coming!
As it was in the days of Noah... So it is today!
We really need to listen to what God has to say!

His word speaks of the coming of the son of man.
And speaks of much wickedness throughout the land!
If this world wasn't spared during Noah... What'll happen now?
God's righteous judgment well fall on everyone... And HOW!

Jesus... The door to safety... Will be closing very soon!
We need to come to him! While there still is room!
We need to accept God's mercy and unfailing grace!
Before his wrath is poured out on the human race!

May we seek the mercy of God, and repent of all our sins!
May we come to him now! Before more trouble begins!
This world is a mess! We don't need anyone to remind us!
Let's seek God's forgiveness! Before his wrath finds us!

God is our only hope! He's a mighty fortress very secure!
Only he can give life eternal and love, that's 100% pure!
Dear God... Please touch our hearts with your fire!
That worshiping and serving you will be our upmost desire!

Only God is our faithful and everlasting friend!
May we all come to HIM, before this world ends!

Jesus, My Life Is Quite A Mess!

Jesus, I come before you! And humbly confess...
My life has been a failure and a mess!
No matter how hard I try, or what I do...
I'm embarrassed when I call on YOU!

You've been there to help, so many times!
It just seems like, "I'm running blind!"
The past seems to be creeping up again...
And causing me grief and pain within!

I need you Jesus! Please help me!
Please come to where I am, and touch me!
I need your love, and your precious spirit!
Thanks for being patient! And willing to give it!

You are the only one, who can restore me!
No matter how many problems lay before me!
I come before you and call on your name...
By your blood, my life needs to be changed!

Thank you my Lord, for hearing my prayer!
Thank you for coming! And being there!

Today, I Give My Life To You Jesus!

Jesus, I've been wasting
my life on foolish things.
Not living the kind of life
that only YOU can bring!

Throughout each day,
how much time with you is spent?
I've never thought of what a
commitment to you meant.

I need to spend more time in
your word and in prayer.
Forgive me of not doing this.
I didn't even care!

Even ten minutes with YOU,
is more that this world can give!
This is what I need to do,
as your child ought to live.

So Lord, my time I give to you.
Take total control.
Make my life new and by your word,
make it whole.

My time with you is
most important to me.
Finding freedom in YOU
and being set free!

Our Society Perverts Us
Jesus Converts Us!

We're all a product of our society.
Our culture comes in many types of varieties.
Many times, there's a wicked and sinful force...
As people forget God and look to another source.

Often, many in society have warped minds.
Many indulge in perversion of many different kinds
We often read in the news just about every day.
Something that another confused mind has to say.

"Where did this person go wrong?" Is wondered.
Another family or person is "torn and plundered."
"If my people humble themselves, and repent of their ways."
"I will heal their land!" This is what God says!

Without God as the focus of our life's attention.
We're sure to go "off course." Into the wrong direction.
"There is a way that seems right." "But the end is death."
This is a truth of God's word... Until your last breath!

Jesus is the answer to any kind of situation.
We desperately need him all across our nation!
Only he brings the love and fulfillment we need to obtain.
We can find everything we need in HIS precious name!

I Need You Jesus!

There's things in my life what went wrong.
I often wonder; "do I really belong?"

During my life, I've had a lot of problems.
I haven't a clue on how to solve them!

There's an important question that I ask.
How much longer am I going to last?

I come to you Jesus, can call on YOU!
I don't know what else I'm going to do.

I give you my heart, life and all the mess.
I trust you now, to take care of the rest!

I need your help, in my desperate hour.
I need your strength love and power!

I open up to you Lord and give an invitation.
I humbly accept your mercy and salvation!

You've given me a new life that I can speak of.
You've done mu more than I can think of!

Thank you my Lord, for helping me out!
You cleansed and changed me all throughout!

You're my wonderful savior and best friend!
I love you Jesus! Hallelujah and amen!

Jesus Changed My Soul!

Jesus reached out and made me whole!
He brought true love and blessed my soul!

He came and renewed my whole being!
He brought joy, mercy and everything!

Thank you my savior! You're gracious and kind!
You've changed and renewed my weary mind.

You gave to me eternal peace and rest.
Serving and knowing you
is always THE BEST!

Jesus, Please Bless Our Marriage!

When I met my wife, what a blessing it would be!
To hold her hand and call her "sweetie!"

From the time we met, my life changed that day.
"I love you," were the words I would say.

She was the one who turned my life around.
My feet were soon "swept off of the ground."

I thank Jesus for bringing us together.
Now I can be with her, today and forever!

Jesus, may your love be what binds us as one.
May you bless us, our daughters and sons!

May the word of God enrich our daily activity.
May it add to our days and longevity!

May the Lord be our cornerstone and foundation.
May we walk in the joy of God's salvation!

Jesus, strengthen us with a love that can't be broken!
May the words; "I love you," be continually spoken!

Jesus Wants Us to Love And Forgive!

A Christian was hurt by someone she knew.
She told him, "I don't ever want t be with you."

She did her best to block and reject him.
Whatever happened, she couldn't forgive him.

She'd tell others of the hurt that she endured.
She was really upset. That was for sure!

The one she was upset with shared some verses.
But this couldn't arise above her "curses."

Jesus said; "bless those who despitefully use you."
This applies no matter how others may treat you.

Peter said; "don't retaliate against others around you."
We need to forgive, even if anger has found you!

We need to watch the words we say and express.
Praying and loving others is always THE BEST!

Let's give all to Jesus, and let him take care of it!
Any kind of gossip and slander, let's get rid of it!

Let's allow the love of Jesus to enrich our soul.
What not of his mercy and grace, needs to GO!

Please come Jesus, and touch the way we're livin'!
Help us to be SET FREE and totally forgiven!

I May Change, But Jesus Remains the Same!

Jesus remains the same!
Even when I'm burdened!
He loves you and me!
This is most certain!

He's the same yesterday,
today and the future!
Because of him,
my life is a "bright picture!"

He's committed to do
what he's promised to do!
It was he, that bled and died,
for me and YOU!

He remains the same!
No matter how many fail me!
How many have let you down?
Can you tell me?

I'm so thankful for his blessings
that come my way!
Words of encourage and hope,
are what he has to say!

He's the lover and redeemer,
of my weary soul!
He cleansed my sins!
And made me whole!

I'm so thankful for him
and all he does!
He reigns with God the father,
in heaven above!

Glory to Jesus in the highest!
Peace toward all men!
He will always be the same!
Hallelujah and AMEN!

God, What A Wonder You Are!

God... What a wonder you really are!
You formed every planet and every star.
You created and put everything into place.
Your creation is a reflection of your beauty and grace.

Over everything. Lord God. You rule.
The heavens are your throne room. The earth... Your footstool!
All of creation groans in anticipation of Christ' return.
We shall get a new heaven. One day... this earth will burn.

God's majestic splendor, this universe does hold.
He's given me salvation... His face I'll behold!
God... who created man from the dust of the ground.
Has given me new life & planted my feet on higher ground!

I love and serve you Jesus now and forever!
I worship your majesty and behold your splendor!

Will You Hold Un forgiveness Forever?

There is something that's of great concern.
It's "The point of no return."

It's a point where a brother may have been offended"
By someone he knows, or perhaps "befriended."

It's a point where something is said or acted out"
This causes this person to be cast out.

Think of Jesus who said "forgive 70 times 7."
If one's destination is to someday live in heaven.

Many Christians get "offended" by many things.
They're hindered by what un-forgiveness brings.

Many who say they're a "Christ-like representation."
Yet are often "offended" by others' situation.

Rather than loving this person in Jesus' name.
Many choose to gossip, judge and complain.

Soon... they reach the point where love doesn't return.
As un-forgiveness inside of them smolders and burns.

What if Christ loved us they way we love others.
His words commands us all "to love one another."

You may be the only Christ others will ever see...
What you do now... will impact others' eternity!

Jesus Is Concerned About You!

It concerns Jesus about YOU,
The struggles and trials you're going through.

When problems in life seem to arise,
Think about the love in your father's eyes.

With every trial, he makes a way to escape.
He's here to help you…Never too late!

When life's problems seem so difficult to solve,
Give them to him ,he's there to resolve…

The future may be uncertain in the days ahead.
Jesus is the river of life and your daily bread.

Jesus Is the Same Today And tomorrow!

Jesus remains the same, even when we're burdened!
He loves you and me! This is most certain!
He's the same yesterday, today and the future!
Because of him, my life can be a "bright picture!"

He's committed to do what he promised to do!
It was he, that bled and died, for me and YOU!
He remains the same! No matter how many fail!
How many have let you down? Can't you tell?

Let's be thankful for his blessings that come our way!
Words of encourage and hope, are what he has to say!
He's the lover and redeemer, of my weary soul!
He cleansed my sins and made me whole!

Let's remember him and all he does!
He reigns with God the father, in heaven above!
Glory to Jesus in the highest! Peace toward all men!
He will always be the same! Hallelujah and AMEN!

Does Jesus Embarrass You?

I've a "brother." I won't mention his name.
A follower of Jesus is what he proclaims.
When you come and knock on his door.
You can hear footsteps across the floor.

Rather than answering and inviting you in.
He won't answer the door, if you're not his friend.
He's quick to judge you. And don't call him at home.
If he knows it's you. He hangs up the phone.

There's many "Christians" like him, who are "immature."
Living an empty life that's shallow and insecure.
Has he thought of the meaning of the cross?
Aren't we to love one another. No matter the cost?

Perhaps people like him serve a "different" Jesus than I do.
They can't seem to say the words "I LOVE YOU!"

Do You Love Me? Jesus Does!

If you loved me the way Christ does,
what a difference it would make!
Perhaps I wouldn't feel
like my life is a mistake?

If you listened to me
and weren't busy all the time.
I'd find a friend like Christ,
compassionate and kind.

The time we've been together has
been few and far between.
Lately, I've done a good job of
messing up everything.

I ask you: "Will you
give me another chance?"
Take time to pray that God will
change my circumstance?

Thoughts and actions speak
louder than words spoken.
May your heart yield to the
Holy Spirit and be broken.

Thank you, for taking
the time to listen to me.
It's people like you that I want to
be with for eternity!

I Will Bless The Lord!

I will give thanks to the Lord, from my heart within.
I will sing of his righteousness again and again.
Awesome are the works of God, in whom I take pleasure.
He is filled with honor and majesty beyond measure!

His wonderful works shall always be remembered.
He's most gracious and merciful... now and forever!
For those who love him, everything is provided.
His covenant and promises have already been decided.

He's shown his people mercy... in all that he does.
His grace is offered to me and you... whom he always loves!
The works of his hands are faithful, true and just.
His words and promises, I can always trust!

His mercy and faithfulness extends throughout time.
He offers true redemption to all of mankind!
Holy and awesome is his wonderful name!
Both today and tomorrow... He remains the same!

To love and honor him will bring peace to my soul.
For he is always with me and will never let me go!
Forever and ever, all creation gives him praise!
I shall bless his name all of my days!

My Lord and my God... It's you I worship and obey!
I love you much more than words could ever say!

I Was Told
I Wasn't Any Good

I heard the devil
whisper into my ear…
"You're no good!"
"Come over here!"

In front of me, where discouragements
of various kinds...
At first, it was almost
overwhelming for my mind!

He promised something "better,"
than what I already had!
He said that if I did what he wanted…
I'd be happy and glad!

I asked how Jesus
could help the way I'm livin.'
The life I've lived…
And HIS power of forgivin'!

Would I trade all of this,
for a life of stress and sin?
Perhaps having a form of happiness,
but no freedom within?

Was I going to trade what God gave,
for a "pleasure of the moment?"
Was I about to make a mockery
of Christ' atonement?

I ran, and bowed my head
and cried…
For a brief moment,
I felt rejected and despised!

I felt the Holy Spirit's
presence all around me!
And then, it was like the love of Jesus
had filled me!

This time, I knew that what I had,
was all I needed!
With Christ in my life,
I no longer have to be defeated!

Satan is a liar!
He has one purpose and goal!
He wants nothing more,
than to destroy my soul!

Take notice Satan!
This is what I proclaim!
Everything I ever need!
I have in Jesus' name!

The blessings from Jesus,
has supplied my every need!
It's an everlasting and abundant life,
that I received!

Thank you Jesus!
For giving what I need and more!
You are truly wonderful!
And are worth living for!

Let's Give God Our Life, While We Have A Chance!

This life we have, how short it is!
We don't know how long we'll live!
Something we all need to keep in mind.
Our life exists for just a short period of time!

From the cradle to the grave, it's so brief.
Do we think about what really lies beneath?
There's more than being buried under the ground!
There's an eternity to think of! Look around!

All that we have, or can ever wish to obtain...
When it's all over... What have you gained?
There's a God in heaven who's given us a chance.
To receive his son Jesus. Whatever the circumstance!

Won't you accept his gift? His offer is freely given!
He can totally transform you and the way you're livin'!
What profits a man if he gains the world, but loses his soul?
It's only the blood of Jesus, that can make you whole!

He is and will always be the choice for all to receive!
An abundant life with him... You can achieve!

Why I Love Jesus

Jesus… There's a reason why I love him.
I've learned to obey and trust him!

He has come and truly blessed me!
Each day now, he's always with me!

He's given to me life that's eternal.
He wrote my name in heaven's journal.

I invite you to come to him today!
Won't you accept him, with no delay?

Serving Jesus is a choice worth taken.
You'll never be alone or forsaken!

He has the power to set all men free!
Let's enjoy his life, so abundantly!

I Learned To Trust Jesus!

I've learned to trust Jesus with my life.
His love removed all bitterness and strife!

His grace refreshed and nourished my soul.
His power touched and made me whole!

Trusting him is the best thing I've done.
All glory to God the father, spirit and son!

The son of God comes with healing in his wings!
He's my God, righteousness and everything!

Thank you my Lord for helping me to trust YOU!
I don't know what I'd do, without you!

Please come and touch my heart with your fire!
That daily serving you will be my upmost desire!

Jesus Brings A Love Most Sincere!

Jesus brings a love that's most sincere!
He's the reason why I live and am here!
He brings a brand new way of living.
I bring to him with praise and thanksgiving!

His love brings a bond with him worth finding!
This love brings a fellowship that's binding!

His love and grace is what I'm here today!
I appreciate him more than words can say.

I thank you Jesus for all you've done for me!
The power of your blood has changed me!

I've been changed by the power of salvation!
The old is gone! I'm forever a new creation!

God's Love Reaches Beyond Me!

God, the love you give is more than I can speak of.
You've given to me more than I can think of!

Your love has reached down and filled me.
When I stumble and fall, it's there to help me!

It goes much beyond my level of comprehending.
I know it's a true love! There's no pretending!

I want to share this love with others as well!
What it's done for me... I want to tell!

I'm thankful for your love and want to share it!
Whatever load I have, you'll help to bear it!

The love of God is the best thing I've found.
Will you join me and share it around???

The Blood Of Jesus Washes Away All Sin!

The blood of Jesus cleanses the darkest sin.
Through his blood, we can be BORN AGAIN!

His blood washes out the darkest stain.
Things in your life will never be the same.

His blood makes all the darkness disappear.
It brings a hope and joy that's secure.

His blood can make a new person out of you!
Don't listen to the lies that can fool you.

Jesus' truth, in his word, is a powerful thing!
He is our savior, righteousness and everything!

Won't you allow his blood to wash your sin away?
This can be your start of a brand new day!

Nothing But Jesus for Me!

I want nothing in my life, but Jesus for me!
He has come and brought life abundantly!

I know that Jesus brings nothing but the best!
With him on board, will my life be blessed!

He's the reason that I can face another day.
He simply wants me to listen, trust and obey!

He's given his word for much needed correction.
He's given me his spirit for help in direction!

Thank you my lord, savior and very best friend!
You've been there for me, over and over again!

Jesus Is Alive And Well Today!

The existence of Jesus, many attempt to deny.
They reject the truth, and accept a corruptible lie.

Christ' death on the cross, many refuse to believe.
They refuse to acknowledge what he achieved.

Christ' atonement and resurrection, they won't accept.
His offer for grace and salvation, they reject.

Won't you believe the words that he has spoken?
His life for ours, on Calvary, was sacrificed and broken.

Will you reject the truth of the Lord Jesus today?
Will you refuse to listen to what others may say?

His message of hope and mercy ring loud and clear…
He brings an eternal life that's eternal and secure.

Let's rejoice together in knowing he is real!
Behold the Lord God! The Lord of Israel!

Jesus Is Worth It All!

Jesus is worth it all and so much more!
It's his presence that I worship and adore.

I honor and bring praise to his holy name!
In my heart and life, I want him to reign.

I bring thanksgiving and praise to him.
I humbly bow as I come now before him.

I confess my faults and sinful ways.
I'll be careful to give him all my praise.

Please come Lord and bring needed direction.
May I seek your word daily for correction.

Thank you Jesus, for all that you will do!
I sure appreciate and am thankful for YOU!

Jesus Is The Only way!

To heaven, Jesus is the only way to make it.
Any other way is simply trying to fake it!

Only through him, can one find redemption.
This is God's truth and there's no exception!

Coming to him is the best thing one can do.
His arms are open. He waits for me and you!

Will you join me and have your sins forgiven?
Will you try Jesus and his new way of livin'?

Jesus is here and offers a new way of living!
It's your life for his, that he's freely giving!

Jesus Is The Answer To Your Prayer!

Jesus is the answer, whatever your prayer may be.
He alone has the power that can set you free!

He alone has the power to cleanse your every stain!
You can find whatever you need in his sweet name!

He alone has the power to raise back the dead!
He provides living water and is our daily bread!

He has the atonement for whatever ail you!
He is always here, and will never leave you!

Won't you trust him to help, in your darkest hour?
You can be brand new by his glory and his power!

I Call On Jesus!

I can call on Jesus again
and again!
I call on him as my Lord
and friend!

I call on Jesus when I have
struggles within.
He's more than willing to
forgive my sins.

I call on Jesus when
no one's around.
He picks me up when
I'm feeling down.

I call on Jesus for sweet
peace and delight.
He's always there each
day and night!

Won't you call on him
to be your Lord too?
There's so much that
he wants to do!

Won't you trust him to be
your friend today?
Listen to the words of hope
he has to say!

Let's call on him and
Humbly confess!
Because living for Jesus
is always THE BEST!

Let's Accept Jesus Today!

Living for Jesus is the right thing to do.
It's no secret how much he loves me and you!

Trusting Jesus is the best way to endure.
He brings a peace a hope that's secure!

Leaning on his arms is where we belong.
Though we are weak… He remains strong!

He's the antidote for our every problem.
Whatever we need, we should involve him!

Will you join me and accept his mercy and grace?
Let's allow is love to put us on a solid place!

Come one and all! Let's give Jesus everything!
Let's bring holy worship and make him our king!

Jesus Brings True Hope!

Jesus is our hope, when there's no other!
He brings new meaning to "love one another."

He brings stability when there's none to be found.
He is our true friend, when no one's around!

He brings abundant life that's most certain.
He's there for us, even at life's final curtain!

His living water is sweet and pure!
His love for us is strong and secure!

Let's come together and join as one.
Let's honor the father, sprit and the son!

Jesus brings tidings of peace, love and joy!
An abundant life with him, we can ENJOY!

Jesus, I Need Your Strength To Continue On!

Jesus, I need your strength to continue on.
Help me to do what's right and not wrong.

I need the strength of your precious spirit.
It's one thing to say and another to live it!

I need the touch of your mercy and grace.
I know that I'll find in you a resting place!

You're my guiding light and everlasting hope!
With you, the pressures of life, I can cope

The strength of your love, I can't compare it.
Please give it to me now, so I can share it!

Jesus Is Everything I Need!

Jesus, you're everything I need today!
Help me to trust you, listen and obey!

You supplied eternal joy and love divine.
You brought peace to my body and mind!

You gave hope when there was none around.
A wonderful friend in you, I have found!

Thank you my savior! My needs have been met.
What you done for me… I won't forget!

All I ever need, through you, is provided!
My commitment to you has been decided!

You've given so much. What more could I ask for!
You've given much more than I could hope for!

Have You Rejected Jesus?

Many have of heard of Jesus, but reject him.
They refuse to believe or accept him.

They live a life, but don't really know him.
They make it known they don't want him.

The things they're doing bring them no shame.
They often speak profanity of Jesus' name.

One day, we'll face God's judgment throne.
We'll be there before God, al alone!

We'll have to answer for the things we've done.
Many will pay the penalty for rejecting God's son.

Won't you accept him, before it's too late?
Jesus is the only way through heaven's gate!

You too can be cleansed and totally forgiven!
Why not let Jesus be the Lord of how you're livin'???

Glory to Jesus! Let The Hallelujah's Roll!

Glory to Jesus! Let the hallelujah's roll!
He came into my life and made me whole!

He brought true joy, when none was around.
He planted my feet on a much higher ground!

I'll join the heavenly hosts and boldly proclaim…
The majesty and power of Jesus' mighty name!

Thank you sweet Jesus, for setting me free!
You have come and given life abundantly!

The hallelujah's have pushed the dark clouds away!
Jesus has come and given me a glorious day!!!

Give It All To Jesus!

What kind of life have you been spending?
Is it one of "wasteful things" and "pretending?"

Things seem to be going "great." You're so proud.
Does it seem like you're "walking on a cloud?"

You have a family. A big house and good health.
Not counting all of the "friends" and some wealth.

Have you thought about who made this possible?
It was God. You may find this as "improbable."

His word says that everything is a gift from God on high.
HE is EVERTHING! Anything else is just a lie!

It's not because of you that you have all of this.
To be wealthy, happy and very bliss.

The next time you find yourself heading toward the door.
Think about what the true meaning of life is really for!

Lay your treasures in heaven and you'll find.
Godly contentment and a real peace of mind.

The blessings of God... Is what you need to achieve.
So the treasures of his love, you'll begin to receive!

Whom Do You Trust and Believe In???

In this "enlightened" day
that we live in…
Who is it that you
really believe in?

Is it someone in the
area of entertainment?
Or a professional team
with excitement?

Perhaps it's a famous leader
of the day?
Or maybe someone
who passed your way?

There are many people
for one to choose from.
I suppose, the "bad ones,"
you can excuse them.

If there's someone
you've chosen to believe…
What kind of real hope
have you received?

Many promise many
good ideas and dreams.
There's a lot who promise
a lot of "cool things."

Whatever you choose,
you'll one day be mistaken.
One day, you'll stand alone,
and be "forsaken."

That day you stand before God
will be the final curtain.
Jesus is the only thing
in this world that is certain!

Flee the false gods
and run from the world's idols!
Come now and get in tune
with the Holy Bible!

It's Jesus that you need
to put your faith in!
You need to put your hand
in his and trust him!

He will never disappoint
or let go of you!
He died on the cross,
because of his love for you!

Won't you come and leave
this world behind you?
It wasn't I, but God's precious
love that found you!

It's on the arms of Christ
that you need to be leaning!
Only he can give your life
true purpose and meaning!

I Took Some Time To Spend With God

I took some time to spend with God alone.
I asked for his blessing in my life and home!
I took some time to tell him that I love him!
I know that he listened and I can trust him!

It seems like yesterday I was a young boy.
There were many things I wanted to enjoy!
I enjoyed prayer with my lord and friend!
I felt his joy and peace within!

I didn't realize how busy life would be…
I thought less of God, And more of me!
I'm thankful that I know a God who cares!
He's never too busy for a moment to share!

He has blessed and renewed my mind!
He's always so patient, loving and kind!
Thank you Jesus for the time we have together!
I'm looking forward to being with you forever!

You're the one that I will daily seek!
I need your direction each day of the week!
All praise and honor to you. is what I give!
I won't forget you each day I shall live!

You've blessed and strengthened my life today!
You're the truth, the life, and the way!
I shall sing of your praises with pure delight!
I know now that things in my life will be alright!

If Christ Came Today

If Jesus came today...Would you join him?
Or would your lifestyle annoy him?
If he came, are you ready to go?
Is he the lord of your heart and soul?

Would he find you looking for his coming?
What kind of follower have you been becoming?
Hopefully a follow of Jesus, you've already decided!
A mansion for you, in heaven, has been provided!

The king of kings and son of God is he!
And wants to take you! For all eternity!
Won't give him your faith and trust in him?
Won't you give him your heart? And love him?

His coming could be today or tomorrow!
You don't want to be missed! And be filled with sorrow!
Jesus is the gate to heaven above!
You can be filled right now!

With his mercy and love!
Won't you join Jesus?
There's always room!
He's coming back! And very soon!

America Needs God More Than Ever!

Across this country, there's a lot of sin and confusion…
As people are looking for the "perfect solution!"
Many laws are being passed of various kinds…
Often as a result of "confused" political minds!

As many in the courts become more delusional…
Over what is and what's not "constitutional!"
When will all of this chaos and confusion end?
As our country's crumbling from within!

We need God! There's no way of getting around it!
Any kind of moral direction? Many have lost it!
God's word is more powerful than a double-edged sword!
Refusing HIS way of living… We cannot afford!

Our founding fathers didn't believe in a God separation!
It's only him that can bring a healing to this nation!
Please, dear Lord, come and touch us with your power!
We all need you in our lives! This very hour!

Only God's principles give true purpose and meaning!
This is what his Holy Spirit has been revealing!
Won't you come now and give him your hand?
And ask for his forgiveness to heal this land!

Please come Lord Jesus and touch our soul!
Only you and make us complete and whole!

Let's Give Thanks
This Thanksgiving Day!

During this time known as Thanksgiving Day.
Let's all give thanks and pray.

A prayer of thanks for everything God has given.
He's blessed us in the way we're livin'!

Our country is blessed like no other.
God has supplied our "bread and butter."

He's given us the freedom, we've all enjoyed.
Be thankful for your food, home and being employed.

For those who've endured hardship... Thank God too!
It's no secret how much he loves YOU!

We find in the Bible... God clearly said;
"I've never seen the righteous forsaken,
nor their children begging for bread."

Thanks to Jesus, for his love, mercy and grace.
And for making my heart, "his special place."

We're blessed by Jesus' love and mercy indeed.
He offers salvation and supplies our every need.

Let's thank God for this special day in November.
Thanksgiving is a day we need to remember!

Jesus Gave Me A New Life!

Jesus brought to me peace and rest.
I am so happy and my life is blessed!

He brought joy in and took the garbage out.
His blood came in and cleansed me throughout!

He gave unspeakable joy that hasn't been told.
He brought a love that's purer than gold.

He gave me peace of mind and hope forever.
What he's done for me, I'll always remember.

I invite you to come to him as well!
He loves you much more than words can tell!

He's the reason why I'm here today!
He changed my life in a brand new way!

Thank You My Lord!

I thank you my lord for everything you've done!
I give praise to God the father, spirit and son!

I praise you for healing and cleansing my heart!
You've brought to my life a brand new start!

You brought to me delight and sweet dreams.
You're my righteousness and everything!

It's you my Lord that I worship and adore!
Each day now, I need you more and more!

I'm honored to receive your redeeming grace!
You put my life on a solid resting place!

Thank you my Lord for helping me to see.
I need much more of you and less of ME!

Jesus Came And Set Me Free!

Jesus came and listened to me.
Praise his name, he set me free!
He listened to the words I confessed.
I was filled with worries and stress.

I didn't know which way to go or turn.
He listened and was very concerned!
He took all of my worries and sin.
He brought victory and joy within!

Hallelujah! I don't have to live in the past.
Jesus brings a love that will always last!
The freedom he brings is pure delight.
Whatever my problem, it'll be alright!

Glory to his name! I love him so much!
I received his blessings and loving touch!
He makes a way in the darkest hour!
I received from him victory and power!

He brings power over habits to be defeated!
With him as Lord, I'm forever completed!

I'm Not Here To Seek The Approval Of Man But Of God!

I don't pay much attention
to the latest poll numbers.
Nor do I march to the beat
of this world's "drummers."

I don't look for the "approval"
of what the "majority" might say.
I've made up my mind t
o seek God's righteous ways!

If many of the people
say something is "o.k."
I'm going to take a second look
at what God has to say!

This world didn't create me
and it surely doesn't know...
What I need is for God's peace
and love to enrich my soul!

Though there may be a thousand
that say something is "cool."
I'm going to be in trouble
if I disobey God's rules!

Here I am today...
I know and have truly decided.
Everything I need....
My God has already provided!

The approval of Jesus Christ
is the only one that I need!
I will follow HIS direction.
Wherever he might lead!

The message of the cross...
will gladly bear it!
God's message of salvation...
I will gladly share it!

Jesus is.... And shall always be
there for you and me!
How I long to be with my lord...
For all of eternity!

I Need You Jesus!

There's things in my life what went wrong.
I often wonder; "do I really belong?"

During my life, I've had a lot of problems.
I haven't a clue on how to solve them!

There's an important question that I ask.
How much longer am I going to last?

I come to you Jesus, can call on YOU!
I don't know what else I'm going to do.

I give you my heart, life and all the mess.
I trust you now, to take care of the rest!

I need your help, in my desperate hour.
I need your strength love and power!

I open up to you Lord and give an invitation.
I humbly accept your mercy and salvation!

You've given me a new life that I can speak of.
You've done mu more than I can think of!

Thank you my Lord, for helping me out!
You cleansed and changed me all throughout!

You're my wonderful savior and best friend!
I love you Jesus! Hallelujah and amen!

Jesus Changed My Soul!

Jesus reached out and made me whole!
He brought true love and blessed my soul!

He came and renewed my whole being!
He brought joy, mercy and everything!

Thank you my savior! You're gracious and kind!
You've changed and renewed my weary mind.

You gave to me eternal peace and rest.
Serving and knowing you is always THE BEST!

Our Wedding Vows

I promise to be your faithful prayer companion...
Through life's mountains, valleys and canyons.

I promise to forever hold you close to my side...
May I walk in humbleness, not pride.

I promise to forever hold you close to my heart...
Till one day, death shall cause us o be apart.

I promise to be with you in sickness and health...
We don't need this world's pleasures and wealth.

I promise to help raise our children in the ways of the lord...
May we be encouraged to daily read his word.

Jesus, Please Bless Our Marriage!

When I met my wife, what a blessing it would be!
To hold her hand and call her "sweetie!"

From the time we met, my life changed that day.
"I love you," were the words I would say.

She was the one who turned my life around.
My feet were soon "swept off of the ground."

I thank Jesus for bringing us together.
Now I can be with her, today and forever!

Jesus, may your love be what binds us as one.
May you bless us, our daughters and sons!

May the word of God enrich our daily activity.
May it add to our days and longevity!

May the Lord be our cornerstone and foundation.
May we walk in the joy of God's salvation!

Jesus, strengthen us with a love that can't be broken!
May the words; "I love you," be continually spoken!

Jesus Is Everything You Need And More!

Where is your hope and satisfaction been?
Who is it that you call your best friend?
Who is it in life that you go to in trouble?
What do you do, when you fall and stumble?

Have you truly found what you need?
Whether it's from a bottle or some weed?
There are many things that will allure you?
So much in life will do nothing but fool you!

Someone loves you and is always here!
He brings a hope and loves that's secure!
He brings the hope to a hopeless situation.
He knocks at your hearts' door with an invitation!

He patiently waits for you to invite him in.
He's the only one you'll find as a true friend!
He'll be with you, no matter what ails you.
He brings a satisfaction that'll never fail you!

His name is Jesus! He's all you could ask for!
It was all of us that he bled and died for!
Won't you give him a chance, before it's too late?
Please do it now! You don't need to hesitate!

The best thing in life is to make heaven your goal!
Allow the blood of Jesus to cleanse and make you whole!

Think About Jesus!

Are you looking for peace and satisfaction?
Are the things in life "a big distraction?"

Are there things in life where you "missed out?"
Have you tried to find out what life's about?

I'd like to tell you about Jesus at this time.
I hope that soon, you'll change your mind.

I want you to think about his love for you.
Think about how much he cares for you!

Think about the cross that he died upon.
Jesus is someone you can always depend on.

He'll fill the void in life that surrounds you.
Won't you let him put his arms around you?

He brings peace and hope to an empty life.
Allow his mercy to remove all anger and strife.

Allow his power to reach out and fill your soul.
His name is the sweetest you'll ever know.

Think about Jesus and what he has to say.
You can be a new person.... TODAY!

Jesus Is More Than Enough!

Jesus is more than enough, for he loves me!
There's so many things he's done for me!

He brings the strength that I've needed.
Because of him, my life is completed!

He's blessed my family and home as well.
We're so thankful for him! I can tell!

He's the best thing I could dream of.
I have an eternal joy that I can speak of!

Won't you accept his love that's overflowing?
The son of God... Today... You can be knowing!

The Cobwebs Of Sin

Many are caught up in the "cobwebs of sin."
They long for satisfaction again and again.

They crave a kind of satisfaction they can't obtain.
Meanwhile, they've only themselves to blame.

Jesus can bring victory, love and everlasting joy.
But his Godly principles, we need to employ.

Jesus was tempted in all ways, yet didn't sin.
It's only through his blood where freedom begins!

Won't you give him a chance in your life today?
Where there's a struggle, he'll make a way!

Satan wants to destroy and "kick you in the face!"
But Jesus wants to lift you up by his love and grace!

Jesus is what you need in your desperate hour!
You can be filled now, by his mighty power!

Jesus wants to forgive and change you!
He wants to do this, because he LOVES YOU!

Jesus Is Who We Need Today!

Jesus is who we really need throughout the day!
He has powerful words that he wants to say!

He speaks of overcoming life and joy unspeakable.
His gift of mercy and salvation is always available!

Hi words of life speak to the heart of the matter.
His words rise above this world's "chaos and chatter,"

He brings health, healing and strength to the bones.
His words of love bring healing to our homes!

Won't you come and accept him as your Lord now?
Won't you confess your sins and humbly bow!

He's all you'll ever need and so much MORE!
To the path of eternal joy, he's the open door!
Let's Come In Jesus' Name!
Let's come together in Jesus' name!
His message of hope we must proclaim!

His message of redemption must be heard.
We need to read and preach his word!

Let's shout his name and make it clear...
His coming is drawing ever so near!

As we come, may our voice be one...
Bringing honor and glory to God's son!

Let's Take Our Cross
And follow Jesus!

Jet's take out cross and follow Jesus today!
Let's listen to him and trust and obey!

Let's come and focus on his work on the cross.
Let's follow him, whatever the cost!

Following Jesus is the best thing to do!
The rest is up to ME and YOU!

Jesus Is Better!

Jesus is better than anything you and give!
He brings love and gives a reason to LIVE!

He brings restoration and healing in his wings!
He's the Lord God and can do ANYTHING!

Won't you trust him with your life today?
Won't you listen to what he has to say?

Living for Jesus is always the best choice!
He brings hope, peace and a reason to rejoice!

The Lord's Mercy Shines Bright!

The Lord is good and his mercy shines bright!
He has come and brought me pure delight!

He's wonderful and his wonders to perform.
He keeps me safe from life's fiercest storms!

He's marvelous and is majesty reigns supreme!
He is God over all and can do anything!

Let's receive his mercy why we have the time.
Let's allow is grace to purify our minds!

Let's allow his love to keep our hearts strong.
It's in God's tender hands where we all belong!

I bless and thank the Lord for all that he's done
All praise to God the father, spirit and son!

Jesus, I'm Grateful For You!

Jesus, I'm blessed and grateful for you!
I don't know what I'd do without you!

You came and gave me hope and meaning,
You salvation and love, I began receiving!

You brought me peace when it wasn't around.
Your spirit put my life on higher ground!

You gave me a joy that's full and unspeakable!
Whatever my sin, it's never "unreachable."

Thank you Jesus for everything you've given!
Now I can live, with the joy of being forgiven!

I Love Jesus, Yes I do!

I love Jesus, yes I surely do!
I love him, what about YOU?

I appreciate him and all he does.
I give him my heart, life and love!

I'm thankful for grace divine!
He cleansed and renewed my mind!

He can change you, if you let him.
Please come and don't forget him!

He's faithful and remains the same!
All that we need, is in his name!

I'm complete In Jesus!

With Jesus on board, I'm complete!
He fills my life, from my head to feet!

He came and his love daily surrounds me!
It wasn't I, but his Spirit that found me!

He brought a wholeness I never had.
Now I'm redeemed, joyful and glad!

I bless his name and hold him so dear!
He calms all my worries and fears!

The strength he gives is like no other!
He sticks my closer than a brother!

Anything I ever need, I have in HIM!
I thank him so much again and again!

The Joy Of Jesus

The Joy of Jesus is a blessing to behold.
It's unspeakable and the half isn't told.

It's a joy most enduring and wonderful.
It brings abundant life so fruitful.

Won't you experience this joy yourself?
I've been blessed to know this myself.

The joy of Jesus is a treasure worth knowing.
Jesus gives it in abundance life overflowing!

His joy is precious and worth the cost!
It comes from victory over death on the cross!

The Treasure Of Jesus

The treasure of Jesus is worth the cost.
He traded his life for ours on the cross!

We're more precious to him than gold.
More valuable than what can be told.

The treasure of knowing him is sweet delight.
He's here to help us each day and night!

Won't you accept this eternal treasure today?
Where there's a willing heart, he makes a way!

He brings more to y our life than you'll ever know!
In him, can you be made complete and whole!

The treasure he gives, all the money cannot buy!
It'll be an eternal treasure long after you die!

To live is Christ. To die is a valuable gain.
We can find all that we need in Jesus' name!

Jesus Is Coming!
Are You Ready?

Are you ready for when Jesus shall return?
Have you read the Bible? Are you concerned?

He's coming back for those who belong to him.
He's looking for those who are truly BORN AGAIN.

He's looking for those who serve him faithfully.
He wants those who love and seek him joyfully.

He's coming back for a bride washed in the blood.
Are you one who's giving him all of your love?

Are you one who's ready to go at this moment?
Have you accepted the Lord's blood's atonement!

Make no mistake… His coming could happen this hour!
You too can be changed by his life-changing power!

Jesus Is Glorious Indeed!

Jesus is wonderful and glorious indeed!
He has come and daily meets all me needs!

He's more marvelous than I could imagine.
His love is much more than I can fathom!

Won't you come and experience him too?
He has a brand new life waiting for YOU!

He's the best choice you could ever make!
Please accept him as your lord, for heaven's sake!

I Invite Jesus Into My Heart!

Right now, I invite Jesus into my heart!
I want to start today with a brand new start!

Over my life, I ask him to take control.
I want his love to touch and make me whole!

This is a commitment that I've decided,
All that I need, he's already provided!

Jesus, you're my Lord and welcome any time!
I ask that you cleanse all my heart and mind!

Jesus loves me and I want the world to know it!
I'm not ashamed, and I'll always show it!

Praise God, I'm Glory Bound!

Praise God! I'm alive today and
glory bound!
Jesus is coming! I can almost hear
the trumpet sound!

I can almost hear the Lord's voice
calling my name.
When I leave this earth, things
won't be the same!

I'll be in heaven rejoicing with
the King of Kings!
I'll be with Jesus! He's my Lord
and everything!

I hope to join the heavenly choir
and eternally proclaim…
The beauty and joy there is
in Jesus' name!

Jesus Gives Me Rest!

I know that living for Jesus is the best!
He provides shelter and a haven of rest.

He gives strength, hope and stability.
In his presence is peace and tranquility.

He's a shelter in the time of a storm.
By his grace, my life has been "re-born!"

I bless his name for giving me much more!
It is his name that I worship and adore!

Jesus Is Worth It All!

Jesus is worth it all and I know it!
I love him and proud to show it!

He's more precious than the finest gold.
He gives true joy and the half is not told!

He's more valuable that what money can buy.
Only he gives a love that satisfies!

Won't you allow him to touch you within?
You can know the meaning of BORN AGAIN!

Jesus, Take My Life Now!

Jesus, I humbly come before you and bow.
Please take my life and all I have… NOW!

I invite you to be the Lord of all that I do!
Help me to daily be more life YOU!

Teach me your words that I may obey them!
Help me to stay rue and not forsake 'em.

Following you is the best path to follow.
I'll enjoy your fellowship today and tomorrow!

Jesus, Help Me to Be More Like You!

Jesus, help me to get rid of what doesn't belong.
It seems like things in me are turning out wrong.

There's some things that I should not do.
Please teach me how to be more like YOU!

I need your words for much needed direction.
By y our spirit, I need needed Godly correction.

I know I've stumbled and failed you many times.
I've filled my life with things that destroy my mind.

I ask for your forgiveness to now be applied.
It's only in you that I can be full and satisfied.

Thank you Lord, for listening to my prayer.
I know you're with me and that you care!

Being more like you is where I need to be!
I need much more of YOU and a lot less of ME!

Jesus, My Sin Needs To Go!

Jesus, the sin in my life needs to go!
I ask that you come and save my soul!

I can only find peace in joy in you alone!
I ask that you touch my heart and home!

I'm blessed for the opportunity to know you!
I don't know what I'd do, If not for you!

Sin causes destruction, you bring love secure!
You bring eternal living water ever so pure!

I thank y u my Lord for listening to me!
You brought to my life true victory!

Jesus Loves Us so Much!

Jesus loves us more than we know.
He died on the cross to purchase our soul.

His blood was shed, our sins he took.
Hs commitment to us, he never forsook.

His life for ours is what was freely given.
That we may know of being forgiven.

Won't you accept his salvation this moment?
You can be blessed forever by his atonement!

Jesus, Have Your Own Way!

Jesus, in my life, have your own way!
You are the potter and I am the clay!

Please use me in way that honors YOU!
Help me each day in what I say and do!

It's a blessing to call and worship your name!
Your blood cleansed my sin and my shame!

Thank you my Lord for this and much more!
It is you dear Jesus, I love and adore!

Jesus, Please Take What You Want!

Jesus, please take form me what is wrong.
There's so much in my life that doesn't belong!

Your way of living is the best choice to make.
I need to obey you always, for heaven's sake!

Please bring deep conviction. I need it!
As I read your word, I'll obey and receive it!

Taking from my life is your purpose and will.
By your holy way of living, may my life be filled!

Jesus Can Change You!

Don't listen to what others may tell you.
Jesus is alive and his power can change you!

He can make a difference in your life today.
He can cleanse and wash your sins away!

He makes a difference in a world "gone mad."
He'll give you a reason to be joyful and glad!

Why not put your faith in him and believe?
Jesus gives much more to life for all to receive!

Jesus Alone Satisfies!

Jesus brings satisfaction to the heart within.
He brings new meaning in being BORN AGAIN!

His words of life bring nourishment to the soul.
His blood's atonement can make our whole!

Contentment in him can certainly be found.
He can fill and place your life on a solid ground!

Why not come and put your faith in him.
It's time to accept Jesus, and not sinful men!

I Need God's Touch!

I need more of God's touch to help me.
I need his words of life to guide me.

I need his love keep my heart pure and strong.
I need to get rid of the things that don't belong.

His touch can do more in just a moment of time.
It can change and bring hope to my mind.

Dear God, please take away the pride.
My life's an open book… I've nothing to hide!

Jesus, Take My Sin!

I've been carrying a bunch of sin around.
Lately, it's began to really pull me down.

This baggage has got a tight hold on me.
I want to do things, but I'm not free!

The struggles I face, I've felt all alone.
It's brought shame to myself and home.

I give to Jesus, a heart that's very sad.
I know I've stumbled and have been "bad."

I ask for the forgiveness of Christ above.
I want to be filled with his peace and love!

I thank you Jesus for doing this for me.
Thanks for cleansing and forgiving me.

You brought a victory that I never knew!
You've come and made my sinful life like NEW!

This same Jesus, I recommend him to you!
He's here right now… What will you do?

My Eyes Were Blind

My eyes were blind, but now I see.
Jesus came and set ME FREE!

He removed the shackles holding me back.
He done all of this. It's a matter of fact.

I was blind to my sin, but this is all gone.
Jesus cleansed of my faults and wrongs.

Jesus gave clear vision and touched my soul.
I can see more clearly wherever I go.

He opened my eyes and healed my mind.
He's there to help and is a true friend of mine!

Lord, Please Help My Dad!

Lord, on behalf of my dad, I do apologize.
He's saying things that aren't healthy and wise.

There's a lot of un-forgiveness that's being said.
He's twisting scripture with his feelings instead.

He's carrying a lot of hurt from his divorce.
He makes decisions from an unscriptural source.

It's not up to us to quickly cast a brother "out."
This isn't what Christian living is all about.

We're to love our friends and enemies the same.
We're to conduct our lives in honor of Jesus' name!

We're to be his loving example in thought or deed.
We're to be there to help those in time of need.

If we let our own anger and feelings get in the way...
We'll have to answer to God on that judgment day!

Let's join Christ' loving family and do our part.
Let's speak in love and kindness from our heart!

Let's leave our past and bring it to Jesus' feet!
Let's allow his loving kindness to make us complete!

Let's be Christ' example in everything we endeavor.
Let's be there to reign with him in heaven forever!

My Dad Won't Forgive His Brother

I have a dad who can't forgive his brother.
He neglects the command to love one another.
He neglects the Biblical way of forgiveness.
He's allowed a lot of anger and bitterness.

No matter how many times he's told "to let go."
He denies it and tells other; "it ain't so."
Yet, he tells his brother; "don't come around."
While his brother is on "the other side of town."

"What is the meaning of this?" I've often asked.
Is it worth to drag up garbage from the past?
How can one who claims to be spiritual be so wrong?
How can a Christian tell his brother "You don't belong!"

What happened to the dad I had once known.
The one who sought love and healing in his home?
Over the years, how did my dad become so bitter?
It's like he never once tried to "empty the litter."

It's time we walk in forgiveness as Christ wants us to.
Jesus really knows our heart and what "we're up to."
We can't fool God, no matter how hard we may try.
God knows when we seek the truth or a lie!

We'll stand before God one day and have nothing to hide.
God needs to help us remove all un-forgiveness and pride!
Loving our sister and brother truly unlocks the key…
To being the kind of person Christ wants us to be!

Let's Walk In Forgiveness!

Let's not to let the sun go down on our wrath!
Otherwise, we are following an ungodly path.

Un-forgiveness comes in various forms and kinds.
It leaves a lot of bitterness and anger in the mind.

Walking in forgiveness is the best thing to do!
It's another way of saying; "brother… I love you!"

It's a way of nailing the past wrongs to the cross.
Christ wants us to do this, whatever the cost!

Let's not bring dishonor to the example of Jesus' name!
Let's not do something that one day will make us shamed!

Let's come together in love, humility and one accord.
Let's come clean n our hearts, before Christ the Lord!

Jesus Is Worth It!

Read the Bible and began to search it.
Living for Jesus is always worth it!

For your life, he has a purpose and plan.
He does this for every woman and man!

He gives us his word for purpose and meaning!
He has so much truth we need to be receiving!

Let's live for Jesus, no matter the cost!
Let's come and kneel before the cross!

In Jesus' Name!

Let's come together in Jesus' name!
It's his good news that we must proclaim!

Let's come together in humble prayer.
Let's show one another that God cares!

Let's be humbled and remove the pride!
Before Jesus, we have nothing to hide!

In Jesus name, we have everything we've needed!
In his name, can our life truly be completed!

Let's Allow Jesus To Humble Us!

Let's be humbled before Jesus now!
Let's come before and humbly bow!

May we come and all seek his face!
May our hearts be touched by grace!

His Holy Spirit is here for direction.
His word gives much needed correction.

Being humbled is the best thing to do.
It's a way of saying; "Jesus, I NEED YOU!"

If Not For Jesus

If not for Jesus, I'd be totally lost!
I'm so thankful for his work on the cross!

If not for Jesus, I'd surely be dead.
He's my living water and daily bread!

If not for Jesus, I'd be in a dangerous place.
I've been redeemed by his love and grace!

If not for Jesus, where would YOU be?
Where will you spend your eternity???

Let's Seek God's Ways!

Let's seek God's ways for our heart and home.
Let's seek the Lord's word and him alone!

Let's do what we can to do God's holy ways.
Let's seek his holiness throughout our days!

Let's find in him, comfort and true rest!
Let's do what he wants ad not settle for less!

God's ways are pure and holy divine!
Let's do it now, while we have the time!

We Need Jesus Now!

We need Jesus now, more than ever before!
He's the way, he truth and the only door!

Throughout the evil, in the coming days ahead...
Jesus remains our source and daily bread!

He's the living water in a land barren and dry!
All of your needs, he alone can satisfy

Jesus needs to increase in everything we do!
He's done his part. The rest is up to YOU!

Do You Know About Jesus' Love?

Have you taken time for Jesus today?
Have you listened to what he has to say?

Have you experienced his love yourself?
I've know his love and salvation myself!

I recommend him to you! He's done so much!
Right now, you can experience his loving touch!

He'll do all of this and there's more ahead!
Above everything else, why not try him instead?

Jesus Is Close By My Side!

I know that Jesus is with me and close by my side.
I should have nothing to fear, or nothing to hide!

His love blossoms to me like a spring flower.
He brings me needed strength and power!

His spirit each day guides with needed direction.
His words of life give love and correction!

May I be yielded to him and humbly confess…
Loving and trusting him ALWAYS THE BEST!

Let Jesus Lift You Up!

Perhaps things have taken "the wrong turn?"
Many people you know don't seem "concerned?"

As each day comes and passes you by.
There's nothing in life that can satisfy.

You wonder each night if life is worth ending?
There's a lot of wasted time you've been spending?

I'd like to introduce Jesus was a way up.
Won't you let his love and grace fill you up?

He'll bring a sincere love to your heart and home.
You'll soon realize that you're never alone!

He'll be a true friend to you like no other.
He's the only one that sticks closer than a brother!

Won't you give him a chance in your life today?
Won't you allow him to roll the dark clouds away?

Only he brings a love and hope so pure and divine.
He'll take your burdens and bring a peace of mind!

What God Has Done

Let's give thanks for what God has done.
Let's bring honor to Jesus Christ, his son.

May we come before him with thanksgiving.
May we honor him in the way we're living!

Let's worship him with our hands raised!
Let's bring him glory, honor and praise!

What God has done, may we remember.
He remains the same today and forever!

Jesus Gives Love Beyond Measure!

Jesus freely gives love beyond measure!
He's glorious and his love is a great treasure!

He's more valuable than the finest gold!
His grace and peace are something to behold!

Won't you accept this loves that's freely given?
Won't you experience the joy of being forgiven?

Please come dear Lord and touch us this day.
May the words "I Love You," be what we say!

God Is Great Indeed!

God is wonderful and great indeed!
He has come and met my every need!

Words of comfort are what he's spoken.
He's mended my heart that was broken!

His words of life are forever pure!
He brings a love that's eternally secure!

Why not come and his love and salvation?
You too, can be a new creation!

I Need Jesus Today!

I need Jesus to help me today!
I've stumbled along life's way!

I need his comfort and direction.
I need the power of his resurrection.

It's in him where I surely belong.
Though I am weak, he remains strong.

I thank him and bless his wonderful name.
I'm very glad he's here and that he came!

Jesus Remains Faithful!

Jesus remains faithful all of the time!
His promises bring hope and peace of mind!

Remaining faithful, is what he loves to do!
Through life's trials, he helps me through!

His faithfulness endures and never ends!
He loves us all and he never pretends!

Thank you Lord for your faithfulness to me.
I know each day that you truly love me!

Jesus' Love Is Secure!

There's one thing that I know for sure...
Jesus gives a love that's true and secure!

His love has no boundary and no limit!
Jesus is here now and freely gives it!

His love can change you from deep within.
It can break the bondage of sin!

Please come and accept his love divine!
Do it now, while there's still time!

If We Don't Forgive

If we won't forgive, how can we be…
The kind of person God wants us to be.

If we're easily offended by our brother…
How can we fulfill; "love one another?"

Christ commands us to love everyone the same.
If we can't, we have ourselves to blame.

How many have betrayed God's forgiveness…
By hanging on to anger and bitterness?

It's time to walk in God s love overflowing…
If it's Christ that we should be showing.

Christ love in us needs to be what others see!
If we're to be how Christ wants us to be!

Let's Come Together For Jesus!

Let's come together as one!
Let's bring honor to God's son!
Let's bring Jesus all glory and praise!
And worship him all of our days!

Let's come and humbly rejoice before him!
As we bring all our needs before him!
Let's come to him with singing in our heart!
Each day we have, we can have a fresh start!

Shall we start our day with a glorious reunion.
Coming before Christ in divine communion!
Coming together for Christ should be our goal.
Being strengthened together, in our soul!

Jesus Lifted Me Up!

Jesus totally blessed and lifted me up!
Now, each day, his love fills me up!

It wasn't I, but him that found me.
Now, each day, his love surrounds me.

His hope blesses and gives me strength.
His grace is an immeasurable length!

I'm honored and glad to know him.
I want all to know how much I love him!

Thank You Jesus For all You done!

Thank you Jesus for all you done!
You've overcome! The victory's won!

Satan's a foe that's been defeated.
With you as my Lord, I'm now completed.

You've done so much for me, I can't express.
You've brought to my life peace and rest.

I honor and bring worship to your name.
I'm glad you're here and that you came!

Christ Calls Us To Repent!

Can God be found in church? How many have sought him?
Is the message of a godly repentance "removed" too often?

He asks for us to repent and confess our sin.
This is how a joyful and abundant life begins!

It's easy to get involved with what happens today.
Then take the time to spend with God and pray.

His word reminds of the important repentance brings.
It helps the Holy Spirit to get rid of so many things.

Won't you allow God's spirit to speak to your heart?
And make today… A fresh and brand new start?

The start of a blessed love and joy that'll last…
That moment you allow Jesus to remove your past!

Let's join together and bring honor to God's son!
In him, a new creation we can all become!

Thank you Jesus, for bringing repentance to us!
We know how much you care and truly love us!

You are what we need in this time and hour.
Please wash us clean of your redemptive power!

Thank you dear Lord of the work you want to do!
We need much less of us, and a lot more of YOU!

A Man Of God Took A Fall

I knew of a man of God who took a fall.
It seemed t happen, when he faced "a wall."

A wall of stubbornness and pride set in.
Before he knew it, he was caught up in sin.

Rather than accept the blame, he chose others.
He'd often get angry at his sister and brother.

He chose to ignore what scripture has to say.
He allowed un-forgiveness cloud up his day.

"Others must be to blame for choices he made."
To anger and bitterness, he became a "slave."

Not knowing the freedom that Christ has given…
He became a bitter man alone and un-forgiven.

"How could this happen?" Was a question asked.
How could this once man of God spiritually last?

Please don't let bitterness reign in your heart.
Don't allow the peace and love of Christ to depart.

Being a man of God requires love and victory…
In being the kind of person God wants us to be!

Jesus Is Why I'm Here!

Let me speak a truth that's very clear.
Jesus is the only reason why I'm here!

He gave love when there was none around.
An eternal friend in him, is what I've found!

He gave me hope and his mercy and grace.
He planted my life in a resting place.

Glory to his name! He rules forevermore!
I need him now, more than ever before!

Delight In Jesus!

There's many things that get us excited.
It's common to get happy and delighted.

There's many things that "turn someone on."
Often, people don't know, "right from wrong."

There's a satisfaction that on Jesus brings.
No matter how hard we try "other things."

There's a satisfaction Jesus that can be found.
No matter if you're on "the wrong side of town."

Only he brings opportunity and love divine.
He is faithful, and has stood the test of time.

Won't you come and accept his delight today?
Above all else, he remains the ONLY way!

Let's come together and worship his lovely name!
Once he touches us, we'll never be the same!

Taking delight in Jesus is the best place to be.
He brings everlasting life for all eternity!

I Love Jesus first Of All!

I really love Jesus the first of all!
He answered when I gave him a call!

I called out to him in prayer some time ago.
He came and redeemed my sinful soul.

I'm so glad for the opportunity freely given!
I've been set free and totally forgiven!

Won't you give Jesus a call from your heart?
On your knees in prayer is a good place to start!

Jesus, May Your Will Be done!

Jesus, may your will be done in my life today.
Help me to listen to you, trust and obey!

May your words of life stir me with a Godly passion.
Help me to be moved by your love and compassion.

May it be YOU in my life that others will see!
I need so much more of you and a lot less of ME!

You're all that matters in everything I'll do!
As I get older, I realize how much I need YOU!

You're the all important one and my everything!
You give me the love I need in my soul and being!

I thank you so much for what you've done and more!
You gave me so much and are worth living for!

Thank you again for being my best friend.
You brought me the joy of being free from sin!

Jesus Gives More Than I Can Speak Of!

Jesus is more precious than
anything I can think of!
He gives much more live than
I can speak of!

He brings peace and contentment
I couldn't gain.
He brings much comfort in the
beauty of his name!

He is so wonderful and more precious
than gold!
He gives unspeakable joy and the
half isn't told!

I bring praise and worship his
awesome name.
I have a new life in him and am
forever changed!

Jesus, Not A Pastor, Knows Our Heart!

A pastor said "the state of the church is strong!"
I thought for a minute; "brother, you are so wrong."
There's many each Sunday walking through the door.
They leave the service not changed from before.

Many are still hanging onto many sins from the past.
They've not experienced a freedom in Jesus that lasts!
Many leave with the same addictions that pulls them down.
A repentant and humble heart is difficult to be found.

The pastor preaches sermons will one "fills in the lines."
While most in the congregation live with polluted minds.
A powerful Holy Ghost service seems to be from long ago…
As many seek something that'll "satisfy" their soul."

Quality time in humbleness and repentance is the key.
In helping us all to walk in joy and victory!
Only Christ alone knows the state and heart of the church.
it's time we really read God's word and begin to search.

Let's search and study God's word in humbleness and confess.
"Dear Jesus, I've been playing church, but my life is a mess!"
We need the help and deliverance of Christ like never before.
In these last days of wickedness, we need Jesus MORE!

Let's come before God's throne in humbleness and sorrow.
Let's do it soon! We may not be here tomorrow!

Holy Spirit, May I Honor You!

Holy Spirit, may you be
honored in my life today!
May you be blessed by what
I do and say!

Come, precious spirit,
please teach me to be…
The kind of person you
want others to see.

Help my spirit to be daily
yielded and broken.
May you be blessed by
the words spoken.

Guide me into that which
gives peace and rest.
Help me to trust you during
life's many "tests."

I need your presence to satisfy
and fill my soul!
You're more wonderful than
I'll ever know!

I Wish God's Best for You!

I wish God's best for you.
Yes I do!
There's many trials you're
going through.

I wish for God's blessings
over your home.
Jesus I here!
You've never alone!

I pray for Jesus to put his
arms around you.
May his peace and love,
daily surround you.

May you listen to the words
Christ has spoken.
May your heart to him be
yielded and broken.

May you trust Jesus like
never before.
He's patiently waiting at your
heart's door.

I wish for you to be blessed
from above.
Abounding in Christ' mercy
and love!

Jesus Blesses Me!

There's something I wish to express.
Jesus loves me! I am blessed!

Because of his grace and mercy for me…
I was blind, but now I can see!

Jesus came and redeemed my soul!
He blessed my life and made me whole!

I accepted him… He extended an invitation,
He brought to me mercy and salvation!

I'm blessed by everything he's done!
All glory to Christ! God's precious son!

He made me a new creation this time!
I am his! He is mine!

All praise and honor to Christ is due!
He has blessed and made me brand new!

Let's Obey God!

God won't give you a job
that we cannot do.
Trusting and obeying him is
what he asks of me and you!

Let's be faithful to him
in what we endeavor…
He wants to bless us,
today and forever!

He'll never give us more
than we can take.
He always there for us
and is never late!

Why not trust his words
and obey his voice?
Living for him is always
the best choice!

I praise and thank him for
who he is!
I'm here today because
of the life he gives!

Let's Plan for Our Eternal Home!

This life we have is for a brief moment.
On the road to eternity, it's a "postponement."
Our life won't be here for long.
This world is where we don't belong!

Our life live isn't really yours or mine.
It was purchased by Jesus! HIS love divine!
Our life isn't ours alone.
We need to plan for our eternal home!

Our life we live was meant to be...
Living with God for all eternity!
Our life is like one short day.
One day, our life will be taken away.

The life I live, I'm giving to Christ above.
I'll give him my heart and all my love!
This life I live, it's going to be...
Much more of Jesus and less of me!

The life I live, I have one thing in mind...
Living for Jesus for the rest of my time!
The life I live, I know will be blessed!
Because living for God is always the best!

This choice I made, brought peace within!
God brought forgiveness for my sin!
This choice can be yours! God's offer is given!
Won't you allow him to change how you're livin'?

Please Heal Me Jesus!

There's something in
my life that's certain…
Lately my life
is really hurtin'.

I don't feel very strong…
I don't know where I belong.
Is this message getting across?
I feel confused and lost!

A message of help
is my desperate plea,
Please Jesus…
come and heal me!

I'm going to tell you Lord…
I really need YOU so!
May you bring healing
to my troubled soul!

I'm going to come before you,
and humbly repent…
Spending time with you
is time well spent!

I know you can heal
my hurt and pain!
That moment I call
on YOUR name!

We All Need God!

Without God in our life, mankind burns within.
Our heart is desperately wicked and filled with sin!
Without God, there is a deep whole and void.
A life without him is never truly enjoyed!

No matter what we do or what we try…
This brings vain imagination and lust to our eyes!
Without righteous living, we're trapped inside.
It doesn't matter how much we walk in "pride."

If we don't obey God's rules and commands…
This will bring a scourge and curse to the land!
It's time we're convicted by God's holy rules!
Without Jesus as lord, we're all a bunch of fools!

Will you join me and confess our wayward sins?
This is where true life will actually begin!
A life surrendered to God is the best place to be!
If we really want to know what it means to be free!

May our commitment to God be true and sincere!
May this be our desire before our life disappears!

Please come dear God and touch us with your fire!
May serving you will be our upmost desire!

God rewards those who diligently seek him!
Let's come to him now and humbly receive him!

Considering A New Identity?
Try Jesus!

Someone I knew believed he was most fortunate.
By living the kind of life he called alternate.

He tried to talk me into choosing: this kind of life too.
I quoted him scripture... He asked "why not bend the rule?"

I couldn't sin before my God so blatant...
When it comes to his word, let's not be complacent.

The lifestyle I have, is the best life I could live.
It comes from God's grace. and his power to forgive!

If you want the most ultimate life, one could ever find...
It comes from following Jesus and leaving our sins behind!

The life you'll find in Christ. brings a Godly abundance.
In his wondrous mercy, will your life have true substance!

There's no closet to come out of, when loving him.
It's a matter of leaving your old life and being BORN AGAIN!

Allow Jesus to fill you with his blessings beyond measure.
Only in him, will you find true meaning and treasure!

Jesus, I Want You To Know How Much I Love You!

Jesus… I want you to know how much I love you!
I want to take the time to praise you!
I want to give you a heart of devotion…
Not just simply go through an emotion.

I want to thank you for your willingness to forgive.
You've totally changed the way I live!
Your beauty shines with an awesome boldness!
I stand amazed at your power and greatness!

You're special to me and mean so much!
How I long for your presence and healing touch!
You brought peace and joy into my life today!
I love you much more than words can say!

You're my best friend. and much more!
You blessed me so much and are worth living for!
Jesus in me... What more can be said?
You're my living water and daily bread!

I'm Honored To Know Jesus!

I'm honored to know Jesus
and what he's done for me!
He came into my heart.
and set me free!

I'm blessed by Jesus
whom I love and know…
He came down from heaven.
and redeemed my soul!

I'm excited about HIS love
and mercy divine…
He's brought health to my body.
and peace to my mind!

He offered salvation
that I have received…
I reached out to him
and believed!

I'm thankful to know that in HIM
and I'm complete!
I've brought to him my burdens
and laid them at his feet!

I'm grateful for his power to
cleanse my life throughout!
He's given me love and joy.
He's what living is all about!

God Gives Us Life

What a wonderful gift from God above.
His wonderful gifts of life and love!
God is always gentle and kind.
His words endure the test of time.

We need his eternal life desperately so!
We need him to fill our soul!
This is the way he wants it to be!
That we could be totally set free!

Why not come to him? He invites you to!
He encourages and wants you to!
Why not start on your knees?
Asking; "God give me more of your life... please!"

Let's Obey God And Not Man!

I heard of a minister living a life of perversion.
She traveled with a message of conversion.
She would tell others that she was ordained.
But her lifestyle dishonored Jesus' holy name.

She preached love and acceptance all around.
She was proud to do this all over town.
This is not true Godly and righteous living.
What kind of life, before God, is she giving?

Is this a life that brings an unholy abomination?
This is the kind of life which brings down a nation!
In God's word, let's obey God's holiness and rules.
Sexual perversion will turn as all into fools!

Let's come before God with repentance in mind!
Let's seek his holiness while there's still time!
Man's ordination doesn't mean one thing…
If the life we live is spiritually UNCLEAN!

It's the word of God's truth we need to seek!
Without his complete word, we're spiritually weak!
Living a life of Godly holiness is the key!
Walking in God's power and true victory!

Let's seek God's approval and not that of men!
Let's come before God and be FREE from our sin!

The Joy of Knowing Jesus

The joy of knowing Jesus is a blessing to know.
He brings peace and nourishment to my soul!
The joy of knowing Jesus brings a peace within.
Knowing that HE has removed my every sin!

The pleasure of serving Jesus is an honor indeed.
Knowing that he's supplied and met my every need!
The pleasure of living each day, in honor to my king...
Helps me to realize that Christ is everything!

This opportunity I have, is a special moment.
I know that I've been cleansed by HIS atonement!
This same Jesus can bring salvation to you today!
He's waiting for you and loves you in a beautiful way!

Won't you take the time and receive him too?
See the marvelous work that he can do through you!
There's a joy of knowing this Lord! He loves you so much!
He'll bless and restore your life by his special touch!

This can be the time, for you to come and accept him!
He wants to change your life! Won't you let him?
Behold the king of glory! Hallelujah to the lamb!
He reaches out to all... With his loving hands!

Let's thank Jesus for the joy that he's given!
By his shed blood... We can all be forgiven!
He offers true love to all and is what life is about!
He can change us now and bring hope throughout!
The joy of knowing Christ is a pleasure to obtain!
We can find all we need in his precious name!

God's Mercy Knows Know Limit!

God is awesome and his mercy endures forever!
He'll never leave and is with me forever!
The Lord is loving and his mercy knows no limit!
He's given to me goodness and his Holy Spirit!

The Lord is faithful! His promises are true!
It's no secret how much he loves me and you!
The Lord is powerful! He's a true foundation!
Behold his wondrous works! All of the nations!

The Lord is coming! The King of Kings is he!
He's coming for his children! To be with, for eternity!
This Lord can be yours today! The choice is given!
Now is the day when you can be totally forgiven!

The opportunity is now, tomorrow may never come!
Salvation can be yours! The battle's already won!
All praise, glory and honor, to God in the highest!
Please come Lord Jesus!

We need you to sanctify us!
Jesus is God! The beginning and the end!
Blessed is his name!
Hallelujah and amen!

I Must Follow Jesus!

If I don't follow Jesus, how can I expect him to help me?
Especially when I have many trials around me!
If I don't read his word, and don't apply its meaning...
There will be many problems, that I'll start receiving!

If I don't seek HIS blood's cleansing of my soul...
There'll be many blessings that I'll never know!
If I don't stop living like there's no tomorrow...
I'll continue to struggle with guilt and sorrow.

I need to change! I'm going to start today!
I want to follow Jesus, trust him and obey!
Please forgive me Jesus, for my sinful ways...
I come before you and give honor and praise!

Please come and change me throughout.
I need to be what a child of God is about!
Please help! I can't make it on my own!
I ask for your healing among my family and home!

Help me to be the person you want me to be!
May these chains of sin be gone! I need to be free!
Thank you dear lord for listening to my prayer...
Without you, I'm filled with hopelessness and despair!

I give you my whole life! My savior and king!
Because of you... I have everything!

I'm Going To Praise Jesus!

I'm going to praise Jesus today!
May he be honored by what I say!
I'm going to take time to give him praise!
I'm going to worship with hands raised!

I'm going to sing his praise out loud!
I'll do it through the darkest cloud!
I'm going to bow to his name!
His message of life, I'll proclaim!

I'm going to bow my head for prayer!
I know he loves me and is always there!
I'm going to share his glad tidings of joy!
His abundant life, I'll enjoy!

I'll share this good news with you!
He offers eternal life! What will you do?
I'm going to try to make this very clear!
Jesus can cleanse and make all sin disappear!

Won't you listen to the savior's voice?
He offers salvation and a reason to rejoice!

You Need A Relationship With Jesus!

We often hear about various relationships.
This often can turn into lifelong friendships.

If you're looking, there's someone you can find.
Too often, this can happen being online.

But there's someone who long ago love you!
He died on the cross, that he may know you!

He shed his blood, just so you can know him!
Won't you take the time to come to him?

His name is Jesus! The king of kings is he!
He wants a relationship for all of eternity!

Won't you allow him to be your lord and friend?
Won't you allow his love to cleanse you within?

Knowing him is really the most important thing!
He's worth more than gold or a diamond ring!

This very hour, you can spend with him alone!
Why not take the time? Even in your home?

Where there's a will, he'll always make a way!
He loves you much more than words can say!

A relationship with him is true fellowship divine!
Please do it now, while you still have the time!

I Think Of What Jesus Did for Me!

I think about where I've been…
It's hard to believe I'm here again!
I think about the many things I've been through.
I ask the question "what am I going to do?"

With the trials of life, bring many frustrations.
A life filled with uncertainty, in many situations.
It's like riding the waves of life's stormy sea.
Not knowing where the next wave will take me!

Everything I have and all I've done…
I lay at the feet of Jesus. God's precious son!
I ask Jesus for mercy and come to him now!
I come before his majesty and humbly bow!

He brought completion and wholeness within!
He's given me a new life. I'm born again!
I love and thank you Lord, for your hand extended!
The beauty of your holiness is to be commended!

You brought me hope, in a hopeless situation!
You gave me your mercy and salvation!

You Matter to Jesus!

Jesus cares and
loves YOU!
He died on the cross,
because he wants you!

Over the worries of life,
he lifts you above!
He does it with his mercy
and LOVE!

With every tough situation,
he makes a way to escape!
He's here to help you!
Never a moment too late.

When life's problems seem so
difficult to solve…
Give them to him and
let him be involved!

The future may be uncertain
in the days ahead.
Jesus is the river of life
and our daily bread…

Do You Have Joy? Try Jesus!

Perhaps you feel like
there's nothing you really enjoy?
Perhaps you feel discouraged
and have no true JOY?

Are you often filled with fear
and apprehension?
Just living day by bay
with lots of tension?

Maybe you're at a low point
and very distraught.
In life's circumstances,
you feel caught?

If you feel confused,
like you're in a trance…
God's word says to TRUST HIM
in every circumstance!

All of heaven invites you to accept
Jesus as lord!
So eternal life with him
can be your great reward!

I've Been Touched By God!

God showed how much he loves me.
He reached down from heaven and touched me!
He expressed love in his words spoken.
I realized that my life is more than a "token..."

He spoke of how precious and valuable I am.
Even though I don't always understand!
All of the times I felt tired and defeated...
With his love in my life, I'm now completed!

God came to where I am today...
Through his son Jesus, he made a way!
He gave me a new way of living so divine!
He brought healing and a peace of mind!

This same God speaks these words to YOU!
Whatever you're facing, he'll see you through!
He wants you to know, He'll always be your friend!
He brings peace and fulfillment within!

He's God! He's powerful and his majesty reigns!
Won't you take the time and call on his name?

Jesus, Help Me
To Reach Lost Souls!

Jesus, may my spirit to
be broken and to you, yield.
Help me to reach the lost souls
in the harvest field.

To preach the gospel
is the savior's call.
Jesus died for everyone.
He gave HIS ALL!

I must not get too busy
in my way of living.
But to learn what it
means to be forgiving!

My life, I give in total
service to Jesus, my king.
The field are ready for harvest.
The lost souls I must bring!

Being Jesus' hand extended
is an opportunity awaiting you.
Reaching the lost souls for Jesus
Is what we're all called to do!

I Want God's Direction For My Life!

God's direction for my life,
I don't want to be missing.
What he called me to do.
I want to be listening!

God has a plan and direction
with true meaning.
I need to open up his word
and start believing!

He knows what's best
and which direction I should go.
I must trust and obey.
That's all I need to know!

I don't know right now,
where he'll lead.
He's blessed me and supplies
my every need!

He brings a purpose
and life worth living!
I'm so grateful for
everything he's giving!

Thank you my Lord for the work
you want to do!
I don't know where I'd be...
If it wasn't for YOU!

Because of Jesus, I have Eternal Life!

Jesus, came and put
my life back together.
He promised to be with me,
today and forever!

He picked up the broken
pieces around me.
It wasn't I, but his precious
love that found me!

I'm so thankful for the
opportunity given.
I'm a new person and my sins
are forgiven!

His grace brought me hope
that I never new!
He came inside and made me
brand-new!

I have a reason to live
that I didn't have before!
Jesus has come and given
me so much more!

I have everlasting life and
joy that's eternal!
My name is now in
heaven's journal!

May I Introduce You To Jesus?

I'd like to introduce you to the redeemer of my soul.
He changed my life and made me completely whole!

I'd like to introduce you to the one who changed me!
He offered to do all of this, because he loves me!

I'd like to introduce you the savior of mankind!
Please think of this, before you change your mind!

His name is Jesus! He's the one I'm talking about!
He's here now and he can cleanse you all throughout!

He's the lord of creation and brings power so evident.
He longs to come into your heart and be the resident!

Won't you accept this Jesus, and allow him to come in?
Won't you too, know what it means to be BORN AGAIN?

Today can be when you can be heaven bound!
A new and glorious life in Jesus, is just waiting to be found!

Through Jesus, a way to life eternal has been made!
His life for yours! The price is already paid!

Please take the time to receive his wondrous salvation!
IN Christ Jesus, you can be a brand new creation!

The Cross Of Christ

Many lost their focus of the cross.
Often, It's true meaning has been lost.
Many are happy in their own kind of way...
Not paying attention to what the cross has to say.

It's more than going on Sunday and singing a song.
It's the cross of Christ where our attention belongs.
A Godly life we must seek to obtain.
Let's remember the reason why Jesus came!

May we have a godly repentance and sorrow.
Lt's look to the cross both today and tomorrow!
The cross of Christ needs to burn in us a desire.
Let's lift up the name of Jesus much higher!

If Christ is lifted up, he'll draw all men unto him.
So all can find the forgiveness of sin!

Are You Walking Away From God?

Are you walking from the God who loves you?
Do you realize how much he wants you?
Have you chosen to leave the one who made you?
The life you have is what he gave you!

Isn't it time to give him your full attention?
Won't you let his spirit to guide your life's direction?
He knows everything that you can think of!
His mercy and grace is more than you can speak of!

Every step you take to God, he takes TWO!
His arms are always there to welcome YOU!
He has a divine plan for your life that's abundant!
He wants to be a part of your life, this moment!

He's God and has a brand new way of living!
Won't you experience his power of forgiving?
Please Lord Jesus, turn our lives inside out!
May all know what living for you is about!

Let's come to Jesus, that he may touch us!
We need his love to come and bless us!
Thank you dear Lord, for listening to our prayer!
Please keep us in your love and care!

Are You Sold Out For Jesus?

Are you a Christian in name only?
Does Christ' death on the cross, sound like baloney?

Is your life filled with vanity?
Does it represent Christianity?

Does your lifestyle bring Jesus shame?
Have you rejected his holy name?

It's time to confess and repent of all ungodliness.
Be clothed with God's love and righteousness.

Come to the cross and be forgiven!
Allow Jesus to change the way you're livin'!

He gave his life. What are you willing to give?
May you give 100% for Jesus each day you live.

A new person in Christ is what you can be.
A bright shining light for all men to see!

Let Me Tell You about Jesus!

Please let me tell you what Jesus did for me.
He forgave me of my sins and set me FREE!

Let me take a moment and share with you…
It's no big secret how much Jesus LOVES YOU!

Let me take a moment and begin to share…
Every trial I went through, Jesus was always there!

Let me take the time to share of his salvation…
Through Christ, we can all be a NEW CREATION!

Let me take the time to tell you all about him!
This can be the day for you to receive him!

Won't you allow the arms of Jesus to hold you?
Even before you were born…He knew you!

Words can't express how much he wants you!
Please come and let him forever touch you!

We Need Pastors to Preach On Holiness!

I knew a pastor who preached on holiness and sin.
He preached on what it means to be born again.
He had a deep conviction and passion in his voice.
Whether you came next Sunday--This was your choice!

His number one goal and deep ambition…
Was preaching God's word with holy conviction.
A conviction of God's power in redeeming man's soul.
A savior's blood that can make one whole.

I'm thankful of the memories I have of him today.
Even though he preached in an "old fashioned way."
I wish more pastors would preach like this man did.
Who could preach and be a Godly example in how they live.

What has happened to our nation's Godly leaders?
Where are the Holy Ghost' inspired preachers?
Have many of them compromised in what they preach?
A way of righteous living…Do any of them teach?

Perhaps the way I believe is "old fashioned" to many folks.
I've heard the criticism, laughter and the jokes.
I'm going to seek God and listen to his voice.
Whom you listen to, for Godly Instruction, is your choice!

Whatever your pastor says, is right or wrong...
God's word in your heart must certainly belong!
Living for Jesus 100% may be an old-fashioned way of living.
But it's his life for mine... Is what he's giving!

God Will Take Care Of You!

Whatever struggles or trials you're going through.
God has already promised to take care of you!
Whatever situation you're in... Maybe there's no way out?
God remains faithful! This is what he's all about!

Perhaps it seems like all you've tried has failed you!
God is here right now! His love surround you!
The situations in life that may face you…
God is there! He is powerful and he loves you!
Won't you invite him in, to take control?
Won't you allow his joy to fill your soul?
Everything that you need, Jesus has provided!
His desire to help you, has already been decided!

You can trust him to take care of your problems!
Whatever they are, he can solve them!
God's word remains solid and is a true foundation!
His words speak peace to any difficult situation!

The awesomeness of God rings loud and clear!
He's here to help and is always near!
He's someone you can give your trust and believe in!
His blessings in your life, you can receive them!

He's here right now! Won't you call on his name?
With him in your life,   things will never be the same!
He'll bring sweet peace and joy deep within.
He will always be the one you can truly depend!

All praise, glory and honor to God above!
Please touch us with your mercy, grace and love!

JIM PEMBERTON

Jesus Can Make You Whole!

Are you one whom bears the name; Christian?
Are you controlled by a powerful addiction?

At night, while others are in bed…
You have a difficult time with bad thoughts in your head?

Do you find yourself involved with ungodly things?
Not realizing the addiction this often brings?

Freedom in Christ needn't be a thing of the past.
While this enslavement to your soul holds fast.

Run from this addiction! Leave everything behind!
Allow God's peace to fill your mind.

Jesus is knocking at your heart's door.
What are you waiting for?

He can break the addiction that's holding you back!
Living by his word will get your life on the right track.

Jesus can do what no other power could ever do.
He alone can set you free. The rest is up to you!

200

We Wrestle Not Against Flesh and Blood!

We wrestle not against flesh and blood,
but powers in a high place!
It's a battle that continues each day!
It's evil vs. God's grace!

There are powers of good and evil
fighting for you and me!
They're fighting for where your soul
will be for eternity!

The Bible clearly speaks of this,
and makes it very clear!
This world, as we know it,
shall one day disappear!

This battle is not ours,
but a spiritual one that rages!
It's been going on,
since the beginning of the ages!

Satan has unleashed his evil forces
to run "here and there."
His ultimate goal is to see you dead!
HE DOESN'T CARE!

Jesus came to sacrifice his life,
and purchase your soul!
He loves you so very much!
More than you'll ever know!

If you see yourself "wrestling,"
against another person…
Let this be a reminder to you!
And an important lesson!

The truth of God's word is relevant!
May it speak to you today!
Where there's a spiritual battle…
Christ has made a way!

He's made a way to flee
and accept his salvation plan!
The best thing you can do,
is to put your life in HIS hands!

Jesus is the best reason
for you to accept him! Won't you do it?
Through the struggles and battles of life…
He will see you through it!

Please come Lord Jesus!
And touch us with your glory that shines!
You've already won the battle!
And victory can be MINE!

Jesus Gives Living Water!

Perhaps your feel as if you life has "run dry."
Nothing that you've tried has satisfied…
Perhaps you feel as if any love has "dried up."
You may feel like you want to give up?

God's words tell us some words we can live by.
Jesus gives living water, that'll never run dry!
He gives living water that nourishes the soul.
And offers completeness to make us whole!

His water is eternal and brings hope within!
It feeds the soul of man, and will never end!
Won't you come and drink of this water so pure?
A new life in Christ, can be yours… For sure!

His pure water can quench the thirst of man.
There's nothing too hard for Jesus to understand!
He loves us so much and is alive this hour!
Won't you drink from his life changing power?

Hallelujah to Christ! The soon and coming king!
A complete love and peace is what he brings!
Thank you Jesus, for your mercy and love!
Please quench our hearts, from heaven above!

The water from Jesus gives life everlasting!
He offers it to everyone! Just for the asking!

Will You Reach Out To Me?

This one thing I am most certain…
Lately I've been really hurtin'.

I trying to do right, but it turns out wrong!
I don't seem to know where I fit or belong.

Many in church just pass me by.
I sometimes get an occasional Hi!

I don't know if the message is getting across?
I feel so confused and completely lost!

A message of "help" is my desperate plea,
For someone like you, to reach out to me.

Please think of people me, wherever you go!
May God's love and compassion flow in your soul.

Spending time with hurting people is time well spent.
It was for you and me that Jesus was sent!

Can God Find A Righteous Man Like Noah?

After creation, there became
much evil throughout the land!
God decided to begin a search
for just one righteous man!

Out of the many people
scattered throughout the earth…
There was only one that met
the criteria for God's search!

Noah was the only righteous man
that God could find!
Other than Noah's family,
there was a destruction of mankind!

God's judgment was coming,
as the many storm clouds appeared!
Very soon, every living thing
was flooded and disappeared!

Because of the righteousness of Noah,
mankind is here today!
Wherever sin and wickedness abounds...
God always makes a way!

If God began a search,
would he find any that are righteous?
There are many that attend churches,
but they must be cautious!

Living righteous for God doesn't count
for the church you're attending!
You can try to fool others...
But with God, there's no pretending!

You're either living a righteous life,
or a life of deceit…
It's only the truth of God's word
that'll make you complete!

May the kind of life Noah lived
be a challenge to me and you!
God gave us his son to die for us.
What are we going to do?

Through the shed blood of Jesus,
all can have righteous living!
May you be encouraged to do this,
from a heart of thanksgiving!

Won't you get on board, the ark of safety?
Why there's still time?
You need to decide!
The wrath of God will fall on mankind!

God will reward anyone
who reaches out to seek him!
Won't you open up your heart?
And receive him?

The loving and righteous
Jesus is he!
He's coming soon,
to take his own, for eternity!

Jesus Chose Me!

It was I that my savior chose...
He's supplied all my needs, food and clothes.
He was there when I was laid off from work.
Satan was saying, "you're no good—just a jerk."

I admit; my accomplishments, I do not boast.
But I do exalt the Father, the Son and Holy Ghost.
If not for his love, I'd be lost… This I know.
This is why I love him so!

He's done so much for me—it's hard to express.
The privilege of being God's son…I am so blessed!
I was a clay jar all broken apart,
But the potter put me together from his heart.

The glue he used was his love for me,
That's why I'm happy and set free!
This I know and hope you'll understand,
He'll do the same for you—just reach out your hand!

When All fails, Look To Jesus!

Look to Jesus in heaven above!
Receive his mercy, grace and love!
Look to Jesus for whatever ails you!
He's the Lord God and will not fail you!

Look to Jesus when there's not a friend around!
Allow him to put your life on a solid ground!
Looking to Jesus is the best thing to do!
Allow him to wrap his arms around you!

Trust in Jesus and what he has to give!
He will totally change how you live!
Believe in Jesus is always the best!
He provides peace and a haven of rest!

His love for you has clearly been decided!
All you'll ever need, he has provided!

Satan Wants The Worst for Me!

Satan came around to boldly tempt me.
He knew my spiritual life was almost empty.
He knew that I didn't take time for prayer.
He wanted me to think God wasn't there!

He knew I had been in this situation before.
Without God, I couldn't take any more!
He knows my weaknesses and faults throughout.
Destroying me is what he is all about!

I'll admit, that me sins do lay before me.
But I know that Jesus is always with me!
The trials I have and deep struggles within.
This is part of a problem that God calls sin.

When I face a difficult kind of situation…
I often get caught in a strong temptation.
I cry out to Jesus when things go wrong.
When I am weak, he remains STRONG!

He gives the power and strength to overcome!
All praise and glory to God's anointed one!
Satan wants the worst. Jesus wants the best!
Please help me Lord to not settle for less!

What Satan tempts as a "fulfilling temptation..."
Doesn't stand up to God's glorious salvation!
Jesus brings healing and satisfaction within.
He is and will always be my BEST FRIEND!

Seeking God's Direction

God will never give you a something that you cannot do.
Serving him is what he asks of you!

Be faithful to him and his divine plan.
Hold on to his word and His guiding hand.

His gentle voice is what must be heard.
His will for your life, will line up with his word.

He has given the Holy Spirit for divine wisdom.
To help show your place in HIS wondrous kingdom.

As you continue, down life's "bumpy road"
HE will help carry your heavy load.

Seeking God's direction Is the best thing to do.
Every step you take…He takes TWO!

God Gave Us Our Life!

Life is very brief, and it goes by fast…
What's done for Christ, is a treasure that will last.

We get busy with our house and nice cars…
Food on the table, plenty of "cookies in the jars."

We often want to spend time with our family…
Trying to live our lives pretending we're happy.

We need to hang on to the shelter of Jesus' arm…
And seek his protection evil and harm!

May our true love be Jesus! Not things!
And enjoy the treasure of life that he brings!

We're empty inside, if God's love we're without,
We need to remember what God's treasure is about!

Won't you come to the feet of Jesus? Don't wait!
Won't you do it now? Before it's too late!!!

Jesus Is The One For You And Me!

Jesus is my savior and the one for me!
I want to be with him for eternity!

Jesus is the one that I need each day.
He's the truth, the life, the only way!

He's the one I go to when afraid.
Through him, a way to Calvary was made!

He's the one that I highly recommend!
He'll be there for me, till the end!

He's the one who brings true healing.
Each day, his love is more revealing!

He's the one who offers hope and security.
In him alone, can I find holiness and purity!

I thank you my Lord, for being who you are!
Your beauty shines brighter than a star!

I bless you my Lord and bring praise to you!
I want the world to know how much I love you!

I invite you to trust Jesus and believe him!
Won't you come now... And receive him!???

We Need To Come Close to Jesus!

There's something that must be a certainty.
As a child of God, we need Godly maturity.

We need to have a godly discernment.
And be filled with God's love. and encouragement...

Time for prayer and Bible reading must be spent.
A commitment to Christ must be 100 percent.

Some may "pretend" to be God's child, like everything's "cool."
But it's God that we'll never be able to fool.

Let's stand for Jesus "in a world gone wrong."
Though we are weak... Christ remains strong.

We don't know what tomorrow will bring.
Living for Jesus is the most important thing.

Let's live for Christ all of the way!
He'll never disappoint us now! Or any day!

We Need To Come Close to Jesus!

There's something that must be a certainty.
As a child of God, we need Godly maturity.

We need to have a godly discernment.
And be filled with God's love. and encouragement...

Time for prayer and Bible reading must be spent.
A commitment to Christ must be 100 percent.

Some may "pretend" to be God's child, like everything's "cool."
But it's God that we'll never be able to fool.

Let's stand for Jesus "in a world gone wrong."
Though we are weak… Christ remains strong.

We don't know what tomorrow will bring.
Living for Jesus is the most important thing.

Let's live for Christ all of the way!
He'll never disappoint us now! Or any day!

I Look to Jesus for My Strength!

There's been things that I'm ashamed of!
I've had more problems than I can speak of!
I've had my ups and downs and valleys to cross.
Many things I've gained and many I've lost!

At times, I've lost my focus and my desire.
As I grow weary and become very tired.
At the point where I've lost sense of direction…
I'm trying to give Jesus my whole attention!

I've come full circle when life's crashing down.
He's a true friend, when there's none to be found.
His name is Jesus! Need I say anything less?
I've found that trusting him is always the best!

He gives me the strength, when it's needed!
With his love and hope, my life is completed!
He's the one I look to! There is no other!
He's a friend who sticks closer than a brother!

Won't you come and give him a chance?
He'll change your life and circumstance!
He's make you a new person from the inside out!
Giving you an abundant life is what he's about!

Please come Lord Jesus! We need you this hour!
We need to be changed by your awesome power!

Lord, Help Me to Reach The Lost!

To God's spirit, I must daily yield.
And have a burden for the lost souls in the fields!

I need to reach others, so that they'll know…
How much God loves them…He died for their soul!

Lord, Give me the words to say, at the right time…
May I speak words of compassion From my heart and mind!

Help me to love others the way you want me to!
Only your love is secure and true!
In you Jesus, may my joy daily abound…
To reach out to others, so the lost may be found.

Thank you Jesus! For speaking clearly to me!
So those who were blind…Can now see!!!

The Love of Jesus

Jesus' love is sweet and pure!
He loves us all! That's for sure!

I need to love him! And him alone!
His love will bless my family and home!

I need his love to help me along…
It's in his love, my life belongs!

His love is what I need to give.
So that others will know, how to really live!

I need more of his love divine!
His love has stood the test of time!

With his love, my life is blessed!
His love means everything!

I'm not settling for less!
I love Jesus! For who he really is!

He's given me his love,
And the power to forgive!

He's given me a love and joy
that's hard to explain…
I received this love,
When I called on HIS name!

Jesus' Gift Of Salvation Is Free!

Jesus' salvation is holy and pure!
He loves us all! That's for sure!

We need to love him and him alone!
And allow his love to bless our home!

We need his love to help us along…
It's in his arms, Where our life belongs!

His love is what we need to give.
So that others will his willingness to forgive!

We need more of his love divine!
His love has stood the test of time!

With his love, our life is blessed!
His love means everything!

Let's not settle for less! Let's honor Jesus for who he really is!
He's given us his love, And the power to forgive!

He offers a love and joy that's hard to explain…
We can received his salvation, when we call on HIS name!

Jesus, Not Church, Get's Me Excited!

It's Jesus, not church, that gets me excited.
Everything I need, he's already provided!

Jesus is the one that won't disappoint me.
Though there's many in church who say they love me.

Jesus is more than a Sunday experience.
Loving him is more than a "religious appearance."

He's than worthy of all honor and praise!
I want to humbly serve him all of my days!

Hallelujah! Worthy is the lamb forevermore!
Jesus is God! And is worth living for!

He is and shall always be the Lord for me!
He has come that I may be FREE!

May all religious idols be "swallowed up."
May the Lord Jesus Christ be lifted up!

Knowing him is the most important thing.
No matter the confusion religion may bring!

Please come Lord Jesus and touch me today!
Hell's gate is broad, but narrow is your way!

You give to me what no church can ever give!
You give me hope, and a reason to LIVE!

I've Learned to Trust In Jesus!

I've been through trials and difficult situations.
It often happens with no explanation!
Whatever I've had or have taken with me.
I've been there when everyone left me!

The uncertainties I've had and struggles I faced…
Have taught me to trust in his mercy and grace.
The journeys I traveled and the storms ahead...
Have often brought stress in the words I said.

Whatever trials I've faced, to Jesus I cried!
A comfort and strength, he did provide!
I know a truth that's important and most certain…
Jesus can take away any hardship or burden!

If there were no trials, how could I trust him?
He's given so much! How much I love him!
If I had no trials, I'd probably forget him.
I certainly know how much I need him!

He's proven how much he really loves me!
He reached down from heaven and touched me!
He's my comfort, joy and enduring friend!
He'll be there with me, till the end!

This Jesus I know, I recommend to you!
He's God and our provider! This is so true!
Won't you give him a chance in your life today!
He can bring hope and take the dark clouds away!

Holy Spirit, May I Honor You!

Holy Spirit, may you be honored in my life today!
May you be blessed by what I do and say!

Come, precious spirit, please teach me to be…
The kind of person you want others to see.

Help my spirit to be daily yielded and broken.
May you be blessed by the words spoken.

Guide me into that which gives peace and rest.
Help me to trust you during life's many "tests."

I need your presence to satisfy and fill my soul!
You're more wonderful than I'll ever know!

Jesus, You're Dear To Me!

Jesus, you're precious and dear to me!
I'm thankful for the love you gave to me!

You're the sweetest friend that I've known.
You brought hope and healing to my home.

You taught me what life is really all about.
You've been there for me. There's no doubt.

I appreciate you more than words can say.
You gave me hope to make it through today!

The joy I have has brought a wonderful change.
I have all that I need in your sweet name!

Jesus Is Wonderful to Me!

Jesus is wonderful and a dear friend to me!
He's given me joy and life abundantly!

He's so marvelous, words can't really express.
The joys of knowing him... I'm so blessed!

Won't you experience him in your life today?
Please listen to the words he has to say!

He extends an invitation to all who can hear.
He brings everlasting life ever so secure.

He brings wholeness to each human being.
He is our righteousness! Our EVERYTHING!

Jesus, Not A Pastor, Knows Our Heart!

A pastor said; "the state of the church is strong!"
I thought for a minute; "brother, you are so wrong."
There's many each Sunday walking through the door.
They leave the service not changed from before.

Many are still hanging onto many sins from the past.
They've not experienced a freedom in Jesus that lasts!
Many leave with the same addictions that pulls them down.
A repentant and humble heart is difficult to be found.

The pastor preaches sermons will one "fills in the lines."
While most in the congregation live with polluted minds.
A powerful Holy Ghost service seems to be from long ago…
As many seek something that'll "satisfy" their soul."

Quality time in humbleness and repentance is the key.
In helping us all to walk in joy and victory!
Only Christ alone knows the state and heart of the church.
it's time we really read God's word and begin to search.

Let's search and study God's word in humbleness and confess.
"Dear Jesus, I've been playing church, but my life is a mess!"
We need the help and deliverance of Christ like never before.
In these last days of wickedness, we need Jesus MORE!

Let's come before God's throne in humbleness and sorrow.
Let's do it soon! We may not be here tomorrow!

Glory And Honor To Jesus!

All glory and honor to Jesus, God's son!
Through life's battles, the victory is won!
All praise and worship I bring to his name!
Over the earth and heavens, he reigns!

He's the almighty Lord and powerful is he.
He's the almighty God throughout eternity!
Let's come and kneel before his mighty throne.
Let's prepare to someday call haven our home!

Jesus is the only way to haven! YES he is!
An abundant and eternal like is what HE GIVES!
Won't you accept his salvation and eternal plan?
He's standing right now, with an outstretched hand.

Let's join together in humble adoration and praise!
HE UIS coming again, one of these days!
One day everyone will honor him as king!
He is the risen savior and our EVERYTHING!

It's All about You, Jesus!

Jesus, I want to do the best I can do.
Help me Lord to be more life you!

I have many struggles, ups and downs.
I still know that you're always around!

You're the one my life was meant for!
It's you, that I must be willing to die for!

To live is Christ… To die is to gain.
Help me to bring honor to your name!

It's about you! What more can be said?
You're my living water and daily bread!

Jesus Is More Than I Could Hope For!

Jesus showed there's hope for me.
He done this by his great love or me.
The times that I feel lost and depressed.
Jesus provides hope, comfort and rest.

He's done more than I could ever ask of.
He's blessed me more than I can speak of.
He's blessed me with eternal mercy and grace.
He's put my life on a much higher place.

As I think about all the problems around me.
His loving arms reach out and surround me.
I pray you'll give him a chance in your life today.
Won't you allow him to roll the darkness away?

He's more wonderful than anyone could know.
He brings comfort and hope to the soul!

Jesus, Have Your Way with Me!

Jesus Wants to Use me. I must let him.
Though I'm busy, I must not forget him.
I need to allow him to do what he wants to.
This is a lesson I should get used to.

Most of the time, 'm not concerned.
T seems I'm busy at every turn."
Help me Lord to let you flow through me.
I need to be your example for others to see.

Doing your will Lord, will be my goal.
I want to serve you with all my heart and soul.
I give to you Jesus, my heart, soul and mind.
I dedicate to you all of my life and time.

A life of dedication to Jesus is what's needed.
Only then, will my life be completed!

Jesus Loves Us So Much!

Jesus took our place with his death on the cross.
He showed his love for us… Whatever the cost!

He alone bore all of our sorrow, sin and shame.
He sacrificed it all, because of the love in his name

He's done more for us all, than we can think of.
He's given us more love than we can think of!

Whether you accept his love is a choice to be made.
You can choose to be free, or be sin's slave.

Christ offers a life full of joy and everlasting.
Your life for his is what he's asking!

What'll you do with his gifts of mercy and salvation?
Through him, you can made a new creation!

His love for you was long ago made quite clear.
His grace and mercy is powerful, true and sincere!

Won't you come and accept, before it gets too late?
He's here right now! All of heaven patiently waits!

Let's Walk In God's Holiness!

We need to walk in God's holiness this hour.
Let's be filled with his righteousness and power!

We need to be his example for everyone to see.
Walking in his righteousness so abundantly.

We need to seek his ways of living and not our own.
We need to seek his holy ways of our heart and home.

Our God is a loving God, but he's a holy one too!
He always seeks the best for ME and YOU!

We are called to be holy! A chosen generation!
Let's seek his ways of mercy and salvation!

Let's decide to choose his holy ways of living today.
Let's honor him in everything we do and say!

Please come dear Lord and set our heart on fire...
So righteous living for you will be our daily desire!

Give Me Jesus!

Give me Jesus! He's been good to me!
He came and gave life so abundantly!
Give me Jesus! He's the one I love so much.
How I wait for his heavenly and loving touch!

Give me Jesus! He's my best friend!
Because of his blood, I'm BORN AGAIN!
Give me Jesus! He's all I've ever needed!
With him as Lord, my life is completed!

I give you Jesus! Won't you accept him today?
Won't you take time to get alone and pray?
Won't you invite him to come and sit with you?
Allow him to come and live inside of you.

You won't be disappointed with him at all!
Won't you take the time and "give him a call?"
Simply reach out and call on his name.
Like me, your life can be forever changed!

Jesus, Please Use Me!

Jesus, please use me according to your will.
Your purpose in my life, I want fulfilled!
Take my prideful and break it as needed.
May your purpose in me be done and completed.

There's a lot of stumbling blocks all around me.
There's many things in life that distract me.
I have sin that I often carry and hold on to.
Please do with life as your ought to!

I don't want to go through life without you.
I realize each day now, how much I need you!
Help me to daily yield myself to you and obey.
Help me to listen to the words you have to say!

Your will in my life I want to be my daily goal.
It's only through you that my life can be whole!
Thank you Jesus, for listening to my heart's plea.
I need to much more of YOU and less of ME!

God Loves Me!

God gave me his love and I received it.
He loves me so much. Now I believe it!

My life is enriched and totally blessed.
I gave him my life and he's done the rest!

He's brought to my life a joyous salvation.
Through Jesus, I'm made a new creation!

His love has brought pure joy untold.
It's more precious than silver or gold!

Thank you my God for giving to me…
Your eternal love and life abundantly!

God, Please Forgive Me!

God, I've done things I don't to speak of.
I've done things I need to repent of!

Please forgive me of my pride.
There's some things that I try to hide.

For all of my sins, I confess to you.
This is why now I come to you.

I realize now just how important it is to me…
To allow you to come and totally forgive me.

I thank you God, for your cleansing grace.
Especially the times I fall on my face!

I have hope for the future and peace for tomorrow.
You've taken away all of my shame and sorrow!

You're the one I need Now, more than ever!
How I want so much to be with you FOREVER!

Jesus, Please Use Me!

Jesus, please use me according to your will.
Your purpose in my life, I want fulfilled!

Take my prideful and break it as needed.
May your purpose in me be done and completed.

There's a lot of stumbling blocks all around me.
There's many things in life that distract me.

I have sin that I often carry and hold on to.
Please do with life as your ought to!

I don't want to go through life without you.
I realize each day now, how much I need you!

Help me to daily yield myself to you and obey.
Help me to listen to the words you have to say!

Your will in my life I want to be my daily goal.
It's only through you that my life can be whole!

Thank you Jesus, for listening to my heart's plea.
I need so much more of YOU and less of ME!

Jesus, I Need More Of You Today!

Jesus, I need much more of you today!
I love you more than words can say!

I need more of your love and glory divine!
You've been gracious to me and so kind!

I need your grace and forgiveness of sin!
Only through you, can I be made whole again!

I need you so much and I really know it!
What you've done for me, I want to show it!

I want others to know of your mercy so sweet.
Because of you, can a person be complete.

Through you, can anyone find love achieved.
All we have to do is to reach out and believe.

Accepting Jesus as Lord makes life worth it all!
Won't you reach out now and give him a call?

God Loves Me!

God gave me his love and I received it.
He loves me so much. Now I believe it!

My life is enriched and totally blessed.
I gave him my life and he's done the rest!

He's brought to my life a joyous salvation.
Through Jesus, I'm made a new creation!

His love has brought pure joy untold.
It's more precious than silver or gold!

Thank you my God for giving to me…
Your eternal love and life abundantly!

God, Please Forgive Me!

God, I've done things I don't to speak of.
I've done things I need to repent of!

Please forgive me of my pride.
There's some things that I try to hide.

For all of my sins, I confess to you.
This is why now I come to you.

I realize now just how important it is to me…
To allow you to come and totally forgive me.

I thank you God, for your cleansing grace.
Especially the times I fall on my face!

I have hope for the future and peace for tomorrow.
You've taken away all of my shame and sorrow!

You're the one I need now, more than ever!
How I want so much to be with you FOREVER!

What God's Will Is

Some get wrapped up into visions and dreams.
They think that this is what God's will brings.

When it comes to God's will, they make assumptions.
But, too often, it's a man-made "presumption."

They often think of God's will as simply "their own."
Have they humbly repented before his holy throne?

Have they actually applied his word and lived buy it?
Living and obeying his word daily… Have they tried it?

I want to be careful to know what God's will is.
I must carefully listen to the wisdom he gives.

Seeking his divine will I want to be my goal.
It's not just something that "soothes my soul."

I want Holy Spirit conviction to come deep within.
May I seek repentance and forsake my sin.

May I humbly lay every weight at the rugged cross.
If I don't surrender to Christ, I'm forever lost!

Jesus, may your will be done in my life today!
Help me to seek your direction in all I do and say!

Only through Godly living, can my life be really blessed!
Listening to and obeying God's will is always the BEST!

Won't You Let God Bless You?

God has blessed me more than I'll very know!
His son Jesus came and redeemed my soul!

On the cross, he paid a price. I'm not my own.
I invite him to be the Lord of my heart and home.

He loves me so much! There's something I will do
I'll come to him and say "I give my life to YOU!"

This wonderful God has done so much for me!
He's prepared a home in heaven for my eternity.

He's given to me life and love worth I have found.
He gave to me an abundance of joy all around!

Won'1 you let him bless you and the way you live?
He's so patient and willing to forgive!
                     A   A
The blessings of God RE FREE ND can be yours today!
Won't you allow him to come into your life to stay?

Allow his mercy and love to bless you deep within!
You too can know God as both Lord and friend!

LIFE CHANGING POEMS - BOOK EIGHT

JIM PEMBERTON

Made in the USA
Monee, IL
24 August 2021

76391634R00134